Responsiveness To Intervention

A Collection of Articles

From *TEACHING Exceptional Children*

Council for Exceptional Children

The voice and vision of special education

ISBN 0-86586-439-X

Copyright 2008 by Council for Exceptional Children, 1110 North Glebe Road,
Suite 300, Arlington, Virginia 22201-5704

Stock No. P5873

Printed in the United States of America

10   9   8   7   6   5   4   3   2   1

Contents

Acknowledgments

The Council for Exceptional Children would like to extend a special thank you to Alec Peck and Stan Scarpati for their continuing contribution to the field as stewards and editors of *TEACHING Exceptional Children*. It is under their leadership that these articles were selected and brought forth to be published. CEC would also like to extend appreciation to Douglas Fuchs and Lynn S. Fuchs who served as the guest editors for *TEACHING Exceptional Children's* special issue which focused entirely on responsiveness to intervention published May 2007.

Introduction

Stan Scarpati

This book presents a select set of articles taken from recent issues of *TEACH-ING Exceptional Children* that establish a cogent framework for understanding responsiveness to intervention (RTI) as a means of preventing academic failure and identifying students as having learning disabilities (LD). The RTI approach has gained a foothold in special and general education due to disappointment with the discrepancy model that has been the established method used to identify students with learning disabilities. RTI is a paradigmatic shift in the way all educators view students at risk for academic deficiencies in that identification and programming for students with LD shifts from an eligibility to an instruction based focus. Much work has been done on RTI and more refinement will take place as research and practice tease apart the model components and test their efficacy.

As you read the articles in this book, you will see that RTI is an interaction between general and special education that holds much promise for high quality instruction for all students. The evolution of RTI and its dynamic and recursive nature might best be evidenced by the unfolding of the terminology used to describe RTI—from *response to intervention* to *responsiveness to intervention* (as this book is titled). Although the shift in language is subtle, the meaning indicates that RTI has broadened its understanding of the qualitative differences in curricular conditions that influence student learning and that the fidelity of instruction must become part of the decision making process. It also indicates that while the focus must remain on valid measures of achievement, the unique learning characteristics of many students at risk for failure dictates reflective practices that recognize that a response (or resistance) to instruction is a complex interaction.

Articles in this book have also been selected because they embody the commendable components of best practices identified by the National Research Center on Learning Disabilities (NRCLD). These components are (1) school-wide screening, (2) research-based progress monitoring, (3) fidelity of implementation, (4) data-based decision making, (5) staff development and collaboration, and (6) parent involvement.

Prior to the articles, is the position the Council for Exceptional Children has set forth on RTI that not only captures the structure and implementation components of schoolwide RTI practices that you will read in the articles but clearly reinforces the critical role special education and special education professionals have as RTI becomes firmly situated in professional practice. Following the articles, Perry A. Zirkel and Nico Krohn in "RTI After IDEA: A Survey of State Laws," present an analysis of how RTI has become part of the federal Individuals With Disabilities Education Improvement Act (IDEA, 2004) and how RTI is allowable, along with a discrepancy formula and other research based alternatives for identifying students with LD. The authors also provide an update on which states have adopted RTI into their special education guidelines.

The range of articles in this book is "tutorial" in nature; that is, they present a coherent set of developmental practices that could easily provide administrators and practitioners with a firm grasp of the underlying argument for using RTI and how to implement an effective RTI model in their schools. We suggest that each article be approached with that in mind—as a reliable resource on using RTI. RTI is centered on instruction rather than assessment, per se, as the starting place to detect student academic deficits. The articles demonstrate how instruction and a tiered approach to service delivery, along with a healthy dose of progress monitoring, can be implemented within schools and classrooms.

First, Renée Bradley, Louis Danielson, and Jennifer Doolittle provide a historical foundation for RTI in their article, "Responsiveness to Intervention: 1997 to 2007." The authors describe how the National Joint Committee on Learning Disabilities (NJCLD) voiced a belief, held by many professionals, that the discrepancy model of LD identification was inadequate in terms of early intervention and instruction-based decisions. Much of their discussion highlights the role of the U.S. Office of Special Education Programs in supporting the RTI movement through research centers and other grant activities. They conclude by noting that the single, greatest challenge to a fully implemented RTI model in schools lies within the general education arena and with the adequate preparation of educators to assist all students.

With the purpose and federal underpinnings of RTI established in the first article, Lynn S. Fuchs and Douglas Fuchs present "A Model for Implementing Responsiveness to Intervention" as a preface to the remaining articles, which show how RTI can be designed and implemented. Fuchs and Fuchs begin with a clear, detailed description of the six components that comprise the prevention and identification aspects of RTI. They also recommend three tiers of instruction as modes of preventing academic difficulties and what "preventative intervention looks like" and a means for classifying responses. Although the guidelines they present for designing and implementing RTI are clear and useful, they contend that they are also tentative, as new research will surely shape them as more promising practices unfold.

Because RTI relies heavily on evidence-based practice as preventative instruction, Barbara R. Foorman focuses her article, "Primary Prevention in Classroom Reading Instruction," on the best practices of reading instruction. These Tier 1 efforts are crucial to the effective use of the RTI model in determining the possible presence of learning disabilities.

The important contribution of RTI to accurate diagnosis of special needs is based, in part, on accurate screening of students at the Tier 1 level. In "Children at Risk for Reading Failure: Constructing an Early Screening Measure," G. Nicole Davis, Endia J. Lindo, and Donald L. Compton take on the issues related to the identification of some children who are at risk. Pointing out the problems imposed by false positives and false negatives, they discuss the importance of improving the accuracy of screening decisions in the critical first stage by broadening the range of data used to make decisions.

Sharon Vaughn and Greg Roberts follow with a user-friendly description of the second tier of RTI. In "Secondary Interventions in Reading: Providing Additional Instruction for Students At Risk," they describe the more intensive instruction and more frequent progress monitoring that characterizes Tier 2, and clearly contrast it with the efforts called for in Tiers 1 and 3.

Tier 3 efforts are further elucidated by Pamela M. Stecker in "Tertiary Intervention: Using Progress Monitoring With Intensive Services." She uses a comprehensive case study to illustrate the instruction and monitoring of a student from Tier 1 through Tier 3 (and later, back to Tier 2) and the critical contributions of special education to this RTI process.

Next, in "Dynamic Assessment as Responsiveness to Intervention: A Scripted Protocol to Identify Young At-Risk Readers," Douglas Fuchs, Lynn S. Fuchs, Donald L. Compton, Bobette Bouton, Erin Caffrey, and Lisa Hill present an intriguing perspective on assessment that counters traditional ways of measuring student performance. In their view, static indicators of achievement are typically taken at one point in time and yield little information about what contributed to the "score" and to how the student will perform in the future. Dynamic assessment, in contrast, frames an understanding of achievement in terms of mediated learning, and these measures, along with the data derived from other sources such as CBM, can help maximize the efficiency and usefulness of RTI.

As noted above in CEC's position on RTI, special educators are taking on new roles and responsibilities and Kelli D. Cummings, Trent Atkins, Randy Allison and Carl Cole describe these changes in their article, "Response to

Intervention: Investigating the New Role of Special Educators." They raise a number of interesting questions and use data from a school district to describe how the skills and expertise of special educators can bolster and sustain effective RTI practices. Links to free online resources that provide information on the foundational components of RTI are included.

The last two articles offer views about RTI that are now becoming more important as RTI gains popularity. Given that the predominant work on RTI has been at the elementary level, Evelyn Sue Johnson and Lori Smith, in "Implementation of Response to Intervention at Middle School: Challenges and Potential Benefits," describe practices at the middle and upper school levels.

And finally, Claudia Rinaldi and Jennifer Samson, in "English Language Learners and Response to Intervention: Referral Considerations," promote a framework within an RTI model that considers the unique needs of English Language Learners. They focus on pre-referral, referral, assessment, and IEP development. Special attention is provided on how to use information on oral language proficiency and academic language in the process.

Responsiveness to intervention will continue to play a vital role in schools when special and general educators cooperatively plan to improve the educational experiences of students vulnerable to academic difficulties. As public policy and daily classroom practice are shaped by ongoing research, RTI will ultimately become a cornerstone of the positive relationship between all educators. We anticipate that the articles in this book will assist in supporting that relationship and promote the development of high quality RTI models.

CEC's Position on Response to Intervention (RTI): The Unique Role of Special Education and Special Educators

The Council for Exceptional Children (CEC) recognizes the impact that Response to Intervention (RTI) can have on the education of all children, roles of special educators, and the special education system. The RTI process is designed to identify struggling learners early, to provide access to needed interventions, and to help identify children with disabilities. RTI is a process intended to assist in identifying children with disabilities by providing data about how a child responds to scientifically based intervention as part of the comprehensive evaluation required for identification of any disability. Special educators play an integral role and have a strong and clear identity in the RTI process. To that end, CEC believes that any RTI process must include non-negotiable guarantees related to special education and the key role of special educators.

IT IS THE POSITION OF CEC THAT AN RTI PROCESS:

- Must be viewed as a schoolwide initiative, with special education as an explicit part of the framework, spanning both general and special education in collaboration with families. The RTI process represents an inclusive partnership between all school personnel and families to identify and address the academic and behavioral needs of learners beginning as early as the preschool years.

- Shall not delay the referral of a child who is suspected of having a disability for a comprehensive evaluation. Children with identified disabilities may not be required to go through an RTI process in order to receive special education and related services.

INTERVENTIONS

- Shall consist of a multi-tiered problem-solving process with at least three tiers (three tiers being the most common approach). The first tier provides instruction through a universal core program in general education until students show evidence of failing to respond as expected to the instruction provided. The second tier provides intervention that is more intensive than general education but less individualized than special education. The third or highest tier provides specially designed instruction and related services, which is special education, and is delivered by special educators and related service personnel. This tier may also include intense individualized intervention services to a small number of children not identified as having a disability but requiring these services that are delivered by specialized general educators and/or other professionals.

- Special education and related services in tier three are based on an Individualized Education Program and use the most intensive intervention programs that are designed and implemented to address individual student needs. Specially designed instruction should be characterized by individualized, data-based, and recursive instruction, combined, as appropriate, with general education instruction.

- Shall include universal screening, high quality research-based instruction, and progress monitoring to determine the quality of student responses to intervention as well as inform decisions about the student's movement between tiers. Tiers should differ in the intensity (i.e., duration, frequency, and time) of the research-based interventions, the level of individualization delivered, the size of student groupings, and the skill level of the educator.

- Shall include a universal screening process (generally early in tier one) that incorporates short-term progress monitoring in response to general education for determining which children require a change of tier.

- Shall use a formative evaluation process, such as progress monitoring measures, to inform instructional decision making about adjusting instruction, changing curricula or materials, and/or determining movement among tiers.

REFERRAL TO SPECIAL EDUCATION

- Shall include provisions for referral for a comprehensive evaluation in any tier, which includes measures of cognitive ability, to determine if a child has a disability and is eligible for special education and related services and due process protections. Data from responsiveness to instruction in tiers one and two shall not be a substitute for a comprehensive evaluation. RTI data does not provide sufficient data to rule out or identify a disability. A comprehensive evaluation shall provide additional data to exclude other potential primary causative factors and inform individualized special instruction, including any accommodations, modifications, assistive technology, and behavioral/learning supports needed.

- May reduce the number of students referred for special education, promote effective early intervention, provide diagnostic information to consider in the identification of a disability, and/or may reduce the impact of a disability on a child's academic progress.

TEAM ROLES

- Shall recognize general educators as the primary interveners and special educators as members of the problem-solving teams in tiers one and two. Conversely, special educators are the primary interveners in tier three or the highest tier. These new and expanded roles in team collaboration consisting of educators, related service providers, administrators, and families will ensure that the needs of struggling learners are met.

- Shall include families as partners in the process, and at a minimum, inform parents in writing of their rights when a student is first identified as at-risk for or as a student who is struggling to meet expected intervention response rates.

CHILDREN WHO ARE TWICE EXCEPTIONAL

- Shall consider the educational needs of children with gifts and talents and their families, particularly related to the identification of children considered to be twice exceptional because they have gifts and talents as well as a disability. These advanced learners shall be provided access to a challenging and accelerated curriculum, while also addressing the unique needs of their disability.

PROFESSIONAL KNOWLEDGE AND SKILLS

- Shall recognize that the knowledge and skill level of educators needed in each of the three tiers is very different, thereby supporting requirements that educators possess the appropriate level of knowledge and skills in such areas as: (1) identifying and implementing evidence-based intervention strategies; (2) monitoring academic and behavioral progress; (3) selecting, implementing, and evaluating instructional and programmatic elements; (4) participating meaningfully and actively in the multidisciplinary comprehensive evaluation process; and (5) designing, implementing, and evaluating problem-solving models that ensure fidelity and integrity.

RESEARCH AND DEVELOPMENT

- Shall make a firm commitment to continuing program improvement through the process of structured monitoring, intensive ongoing evaluation, and systemic professional training based on evolving research and practice.

- Shall consider the intended and unintended consequences of moving toward more wide-scale implementation without more extensive research and development efforts that clearly demonstrate effectiveness in improving the achievement of students with exceptionalities over time.

- Shall engage in research and development to inform practice, particularly in the areas of implementation across all academic and/or behavioral areas and age levels; movement back and forth from tiers and data needed to understand this movement; the use of tiers one and two data to help inform the identification of a disability; the problem solving and standard treatment protocol approaches to instruction; and the conceptual issues associated with nonresponsiveness; and measuring and defining nonresponsiveness.

RESOURCES

- Shall ensure that sufficient resources are available to cover a substantial percentage of the costs that state, provincial, and local jurisdictions will incur to implement and institutionalize this initiative without reducing expenditures for other education programs.

To access CEC's Position on Response to Intervention online, go to www.cec.sped.org > Policy & Advocacy > CEC Professional Policies. For further information, contact Deborah A. Ziegler, Associate Executive Director, Policy and Advocacy Services, Council for Exceptional Children, 703-264-9406 (P), 703-243-0410 (F), 800-224-6830 (Toll free), 866-915-5000 (TTY), debz@cec.sped.org.

Responsiveness to Intervention: 1997 to 2007

Renée Bradley, Louis Danielson, and Jennifer Doolittle

THE OSEP LEARNING DISABILITIES INITIATIVE

In 1997, during the process of reauthorizing the Individuals with Disabilities Education Act (IDEA), the National Joint Committee on Learning Disabilities (NJCLD) wrote a letter to the U.S. Office of Special Education Programs (OSEP) expressing concern that neither early nor accurate identification of specific learning disabilities (SLD) was occurring (NJCLD, 1997). The activities that followed the response from OSEP to the NJCLD letter have become known as the Learning Disabilities, or LD, Initiative (Bradley & Danielson, 2004). The LD Initiative began as a comprehensive attempt to bring researchers, professional organizations, advocacy groups, educators, and other stakeholders to a consensus regarding the identification and implementation of improved procedures for SLD identification. The goal of the LD Initiative was to improve the process and ensure accurate and efficient identification of students with SLD. Reliance on the use of the discrepancy approach to determine eligibility for special education services had resulted in students with SLD not being identified until they had experienced multiple years of failure. Additionally, this approach provided teachers little information on which they could base instructional decisions.

The purpose of this article is to provide: (a) a brief description of the conclusions of the LD Initiative and the impact these conclusions have had, (b) an overview of the new regulations regarding response to intervention (RTI) and the identification of children with SLD, and (c) information about current technical-assistance activities.

Early in the work of the LD Initiative, RTI emerged as a concept worthy of investigation. One of the original consensus statements from the collaborative work on the LD Initiative stated:

> There should be alternate ways to identify individuals with SLD in addition to achievement testing, history, and observations of the child. Response to quality intervention is the most promising method of alternate identification and can both promote effective practices in schools and help to close the gap between identification and treatment (Bradley, Danielson, & Hallahan, 2002).

One reason that RTI was a welcome alternative to the traditional discrepancy approach is that teachers no longer would have to wait for students to fail before the students could receive services. RTI begins with the implementation of scientifically based, schoolwide instructional interventions and promotes intervention at the first indication of nonresponse to traditional classroom instruction. In addition, RTI is consistent with a shift of emphasis from process to outcomes for students with disabilities. This shift is viewed as important both practically and theoretically for the field of SLD—which historically has concentrated more on the search for the specific condition of SLD and its cause than on intervention effectiveness (Bradley, Danielson, & Doolittle, 2005; Ysseldyke, 2002).

The early collaborative work associated with the OSEP LD Initiative made it possible for all stakeholders—including parents, researchers, and other professionals—to move forward and focus on operationalizing the implementation of RTI. In 2001, recognizing the increasing need for RTI-related research, information, and technical assistance, OSEP funded the National Research Center on Learning Disabilities (NRCLD). NRCLD was given the challenging tasks of investigating the effects and impact of a variety of proposed SLD identification methods, identifying potential models of RTI, and developing technical assistance documents to assist states and local entities with the anticipated change in SLD identification procedures. The work of NRCLD was taken into consideration in the process of creating the amendments to the Individuals With Disabilities Education Act (IDEA) in 2004.

The 2004 reauthorization of IDEA effectively removed the longstanding federal requirement to use the aptitude/achievement discrepancy for identification of SLD, and it now permits RTI to be used as an approach for identification. The amendments to IDEA specifically state that "a local educational agency (LEA) may use a process that determines if the child responds to scientific, research-based intervention as a part of the evaluation procedures." [§ 614(b)(6)(A-B, IDEA 2004)]. This language, combined with other work of the OSEP LD Initiative, led many states to investigate RTI as an approach for SLD identification.

A FRAMEWORK FOR RTI

There are many RTI models being implemented in schools and districts across the country. No one model has emerged as the model of choice, and the U.S. Department of Education (the Department) does not recommend or endorse any one specific model. In the analysis of comments for the IDEA regulations, the Department reinforced the flexibility provided in the regulations regarding RTI stating:

> New §300.307(a)(3) [(proposed §300.307(a)(4)] recognizes that there are alternative models to identify children with SLD that are based on sound scientific research and gives States flexibility to use these models. For example, a State could choose to identify children based on absolute low achievement and consideration of exclusionary factors as one criterion for eligibility. Other alternatives might combine features of different models for identification. We believe the evaluation procedures in section 614(b)(2) and (b)(3) of the Act give the Department the flexibility to allow States to use alternative, research-based procedures for determining whether a child has an SLD and is eligible for special education and related services. (USED 2006, 46648)

Although the Department has not endorsed a single model, there is a basic framework of RTI emerging in research and practice that is common to the most prevalent models. RTI has been conceptualized as a multi-tiered prevention model that has at least three tiers. The first tier, referred to as primary intervention, consists of high-quality, research-based instruction in the general education setting, universal screening to identify at-risk students, and progress monitoring to detect those students who might not be responding to this primary intervention as expected. Within this multi-tiered framework, decisions regarding movement from one level to the next are based on the quality of student responses to research-based interventions. Subsequent levels differ in intensity (i.e., duration, frequency, and time) of the research-based interventions being delivered, the size of the student groupings, and the skill level of the service provider. These secondary interventions typically are 8 to 12 weeks in duration. Findings from NRCLD indicate that the length of time needed for the second tier can vary, but generally it should not exceed 8 weeks. Eight weeks is an adequate amount of time to realize the response or lack of response of a student to a well-matched evidence-based intervention (Cortiella, 2006).

The final—or tertiary—level consists of individualized and intensive interventions and services, which might or might not be similar to traditional special education services. In most models, the lack of appropriate response to the more intensive and more individualized research-based instruction at this tertiary tier results in referral for a full and individual evaluation under IDEA. The quality and amount of information collected through progress monitoring of a student's response to interventions through the previous tiers can provide extremely useful data for the team charged with determining eligibility of a student for special education services.

In 2002, NRCLD initiated a process to identify and record the work and outcomes of a group of potential model RTI sites around the country. Although no one site emerged as a complete "model" that addressed all critical elements identified by NRCLD, there were a group of sites that distinguished themselves by exhibiting many of the critical elements, such as: (a) implementation of a research-based core reading program, (b) universal screening for at-risk students, (c) continuous progress monitoring at the secondary and subsequent tiers, and (d) a combination of a problem-solving model and the use of a standard protocol. All of the sites, however, lacked specific data on fidelity of implementation of the interventions and specific details regarding decision making on responsiveness to the interventions.

One outcome derived from analyzing these sites' RTI models was the ability to characterize the features of an RTI model that is successfully implemented in a school setting. In a school with a well-functioning RTI model: (a) students receive high-quality, research-based instruction from qualified staff in their general education setting; (b) general education staff members assume an active role in students' assessment in the curriculum; (c) school staff conducts universal screening of academics and behavior; (d) school staff implements specific, research-based interventions to address the students' difficulties; (e) school staff conducts continuous progress monitoring of student performance (i.e., weekly or biweekly) for secondary and tertiary interventions and less frequently in general education; (f) school staff uses progress monitoring data and explicit decision rules to determine interventions' effectiveness and necessary modifications; (g) systematic assessment is made regarding the fidelity or integrity with which instruction and interventions are implemented; and (h) the RTI model includes, as required, provisions for referral for comprehensive evaluation, free appropriate public education, and due process protections (National Research Center on Learning Disabilities, 2006).

IDEA REGULATORY GUIDANCE

As noted, the statutory reference to RTI is brief. In comments responding to the Notice for Proposed Rule Making for the IDEA federal regulations (USED, 2005), RTI ranked among the top-three issues in the number of comments received (USED, 2006). The majority of comments spoke to the need for more direction regarding the identification of children with SLD, the implementation of RTI, and clarification as to how RTI fits within the existing evaluation and procedural safeguards (USED, 2006). In August 2006, the IDEA regulatory guidance was published. The following section describes the key issues addressed in the regulations including evaluation for SLD, RTI definition, parental notice, and LEA request for evaluation. This information is intended to supplement and not to replace careful study and application of IDEA and its regulations.

In evaluating a child with SLD, the state criteria must not require the use of a severe discrepancy between intellectual ability and achievement and the criteria must permit the use of a process based on the child's response to scientific, research-based intervention. These state criteria must be used by public agencies in determining whether a child has an SLD. Certain standards for evaluation using RTI are presented in the regulations. One aspect that must be examined when determining the existence of SLD is whether the child is making sufficient progress for the child's age or to meet state-approved grade-level standards. Another facet is ensuring that underachievement in a child suspected of having a SLD is not due to the lack of appropriate instruction in reading or math.

Additionally, the regulations do not define RTI but instead state that there are many RTI models. Accordingly, the regulations are written to accommodate the many different models that are currently in use. Although the Department does not mandate or endorse any particular model, the regulations mandate that states permit the use of a process, based on the child's response to scientific, research-based intervention [USED, 2006 §300.307(a)(2)]. Although many of the specific procedures to be used are not defined in either IDEA or its regulatory guidance, the importance of timelines and structured communication with parents is emphasized.

Regarding parental notice, the regulations state that the public agency must promptly request parental consent to evaluate the child to determine if the child needs special education and related services and must adhere to the timeframes described in §§300.301 and 300.303. Parent consent must be requested if, prior to a referral, a child has not made adequate progress after an appropriate period of time when provided instruction as described in the regulations, or when the child is referred for evaluation [USED, 2006 §300.307(c)]. The regulations recognize that instructional models vary in terms of the frequency and number of repeated assessments that are required to determine a child's progress; accordingly, states may create criteria that take local variation into consideration.

Regarding the comprehensive evaluation, the regulations are clear that RTI is not a substitute for a comprehensive evaluation. A variety of data-gathering and assessment tools and strategies must be used even if an RTI model has been implemented. No single procedure can be relied on as the sole criterion for determining eligibility for special education services. Each state must develop criteria to determine whether a child has a disability and RTI can be one component of the information reviewed (USED, 2006, 46648).

MOVING TOWARDS LARGE-SCALE IMPLEMENTATION

As schools, districts, and states move toward more wide-scale implementation of RTI, multiple challenges remain. The greatest challenge in implementing

RTI is the limited experience of doing so on a large scale, across all academic areas and age levels. Even with these gaps in knowledge, however, there is evidence supporting RTI as an improvement over past identification models. The Analysis of Comments addresses this issue:

> There is an evidence base to support the use of RTI models to identify children with SLD on a wide scale, including young children and children from minority backgrounds. These include several large-scale implementations in Iowa (the Heartland model; Tilly, 2002); the Minneapolis public schools (Marston, 2003); applications of the Screening to Enhance Equitable Placement (STEEP) model in Mississippi, Louisiana, and Arizona (VanDerHeyden, Witt, & Gilbertson, in press); and other examples (NASDE, 2005). While it is true that much of the research on RTI models has been conducted in the area of reading, 80 to 90 percent of children with SLD experience reading problems. The implementation of RTI in practice, however, has included other domains. (USED, 2005 46647)

Ideally, large-scale implementation of any new innovation would be preceded by significant research and development efforts. The reality, however, is that policy often precedes and drives research and development. In addition to RTI, policy has preceded a large body of evidence in the areas of assessment, access to the general curriculum, and discipline issues (Danielson, Doolittle, & Bradley, 2005).

Given that most students with disabilities (93.6%) spend at least part of each school day in a general education classroom—an average of 4.8 hours per day (Wagner & Blackorby, 2002)—the greatest challenge of scaling-up RTI could rest largely in the general education arena. The preparation of all educators to assist all students, including those with disabilities, in meaningfully accessing the general curriculum becomes a critical component of successful large-scale implementation. Further discussion is also needed regarding implementation of the model in middle school and high school, the use of RTI in content areas other than early reading, and the role of parents in the process. Currently, the momentum around the potential benefits of RTI has created a critical mass of professionals willing to forge ahead despite the unanswered questions surrounding the details of implementation.

OSEP is committed to the provision of technical assistance to assist states in the implementation of RTI. NRCLD continues to provide information to enhance implementation strategies and soon will release a resource kit with information for implementers and families. OSEP is also collaborating with (and co-funded) the Comprehensive Center on Instruction—overseen by the U.S. Office of Elementary and Secondary Education—to embed RTI information and developments within the general education framework. OSEP also has a variety of information available on RTI as part of the recent IDEA Part B regulation rollout activities that can be accessed at http://idea.ed.gov. As further implementation strategies and outcome data accrue, OSEP continues to work with the technical assistance centers, parent training centers, state educational agencies, and other governmental offices to ensure that educators, administrators, and parents are well informed about RTI.

Nearly 10 years ago, the professional organizations involved in improving services for children with SLD elevated the discussion of the need to develop more accurate and efficient processes for the identification of these students to a national level. The 2004 reauthorized IDEA and guidance in the subsequent regulations, as well as the wealth of information being generated from NRCLD and other centers on how to proceed in implementing RTI, have helped create a great opportunity to improve the identification of, and services for, children with SLD. Even more exciting is the current chance to infuse strategies and interventions that traditionally are used only in special education—such as progress monitoring—into the day-to-day practice of general education. Success in this venture could improve instruction and learning for many children, those with and without disabilities.

For more information on RTI and the IDEA federal regulations, please visit The National Research Center on Learning Disabilities Web site at http://www.NRCLD.org, and the Department's IDEA regulation Web site at http://idea.ed.gov.

REFERENCES

Bradley, R., & Danielson, L. (2004). Office of Special Education Program's LD initiative: A context for inquiry and consensus. *Learning Disability Quarterly, 27*(4), 186–188.

Bradley, R., Danielson, L., & Doolittle, J. (2005). Response to Intervention. *Journal of Learning Disabilities, 38*(6), 485–486.

Bradley, R., Danielson, L., & Hallahan, D. (2002). *Identification of learning disabilities: Research to practice.* Mahwah, NJ: Lawrence Erlbaum.

Cortiella, C. (2006). A parent's guide to response-to-intervention [Web site]. Retrieved January 12, 2007, from http://www.ncld.org/images/stories/downloads/parent_center/rti_final.pdf

Danielson, L., Doolittle, J., & Bradley, R. (2005). Past accomplishments and future challenges. *Learning Disability Quarterly, 28*(2), 137–139.

Individuals With Disabilities Education Act of 2004 (IDEA 2004), Public Law 108-446, 108th Congress. Dec. 3, 2004. Available through http://idea.ed.gov/explore/home (accessed Feb. 14, 2007).

National Joint Committee on Learning Disabilities (NJCLD). (1997). As cited in U.S. Department of Education, "Assistance to States for the Education of Children With Disabilities, Preschool Grants for Children With Disabilities, and Early Intervention Program for Infants and Toddlers With Disabilities; Proposed Rule," 34 CFR 300, 301, and 303, Federal Register 62: 204 (Oct. 22, 1997). Available at: http://www.ed.gov/legislation/Fed   Register/proprule/1997-4/102297a.html (accessed March 5, 2007).

National Research Center on Learning Disabilities. (2006). Core concepts of RTI [Web site]. Retrieved January 12, 2007, from http://www.nrcld.org/research/rti/concepts.shtml

U.S. Department of Education (USED). (2005). "Assistance to States for the Education of Children With Disabilities and Preschool Grants for Children With Disabilities; Proposed Rule," 34 CFR Parts 300, 301, and 304, Federal Register 70:118 (June 21, 2005): 35781-35892. Available at: http//www.ed.gov/legislation/Fed Register/proprule/2005-2/062105a.html (accessed February 14, 2007).

U.S. Department of Education (USED) (2006). "Assistance to States for the Education of Children With Disabilities and Preschool Grants for Children With Disabilities: Final Rule," 34 CFR Parts 300 and 301, *Federal Register* 71:156 (Aug. 14, 2006): 46540–46845. Available at: http://www.idea.ed.gov/download/finalregulations.pdr (accessed February 14, 2007).

Wagner, R., & Blackorby, J. (2002). *Disability profiles of elementary and middle school students with disabilities: Special Education Elementary Longitudinal Study (SEELS)*. Palo Alto, CA: SRI International.

Ysseldyke, J. (2002). Response to "Learning disabilities: Historical perspectives." In R. Bradley, L. Danielson, & D. P. Hallahan (Eds.), *Identification of learning disabilities: Research to practice* (pp. 89–98). Mahwah, NJ: Lawrence Erlbaum.

Opinions expressed herein are those of the authors and do not necessarily reflect the position or policies of the U.S. Office of Special Education Programs or the U.S. Department of Education, and no official endorsement by the government should be inferred.

Originally published in *TEACHING Exceptional Children*, Vol. 39, No. 5, pp. 8–12.

3

A Model for Implementing Responsiveness to Intervention

Lynn S. Fuchs and Douglas Fuchs

For decades, the major procedure for identifying children with learning disabilities (LD) has involved documenting a discrepancy between a student's IQ and achievement. With this approach, however, identification typically occurs at fifth grade, so children must "wait-to-fail" before intervention can occur. For this reason, along with technical difficulties associated with the IQ-achievement discrepancy (see Vaughn & Fuchs, 2003 for a summary), the 2004 reauthorization of the Individuals With Disabilities Education Improvement Act (P.L. 108-446) permits states to discontinue use of IQ-achievement discrepancy in favor of Response to Intervention (RTI) for LD identification. Advantages of RTI include earlier identification, a stronger focus on prevention, and assessment with clearer implications for academic programming (Vaughn & Fuchs). The premise behind RTI is that students are identified as LD when their response to validated intervention is dramatically inferior to that of peers. The inference is that these children who respond poorly to generally effective interventions have a disability that requires specialized treatment to produce successful learning outcomes. In this way, a central assumption is that RTI can differentiate between two explanations for low achievement: inadequate instruction versus disability. If the child responds poorly to instruction that benefits most students, then the assessment eliminates instructional quality as a viable explanation for poor academic growth and instead provides evidence of disability. Also, because most children respond nicely to validated intervention, RTI serves an important prevention function.

Most RTI models of LD identification are embedded within a multi-tier prevention system (see Figure 1). General education constitutes primary prevention. Students who fail to respond to this "universal" core program enter the RTI LD identification process with secondary prevention. In most research studies, this involves one or more rounds of research-based small-group tutoring. Students who respond poorly to this more intensive form of prevention are considered to have demonstrated "unexpected failure" and become candidates for tertiary intervention. They then undergo an instructionally focused multi-disciplinary evaluation, designed to answer questions that arose during primary and secondary prevention and to eliminate other forms of disability as a cause for failure (if another disability is suspected). Tertiary prevention is the most intensive form of instruction, involving individualized programming in conjunction with progress monitoring. When adequate performance is achieved, the child exits to secondary or primary prevention. In this way, RTI has two goals: (a) to identify risk early so that students participate in prevention prior to the onset of severe deficits, which can be difficult to remediate, and (b) to identify students with LD who prove unresponsive to validated, standardized forms of instruction and instead require an individualized form of instruction.

As schools consider implementing RTI, they must make decisions about how to operationalize six components constituting the RTI process. In this article, we describe options for each component. Then, we offer our best thinking, in light of the research evidence to date, about how schools might proceed. Finally, we describe what an RTI system might look like at first grade in reading and in math when our recommendations are adopted.

SIX RTI COMPONENTS

To implement RTI for prevention and identification, schools must make decisions about six components that constitute the process: how many tiers of intervention to use, how to target students for preventative intervention, the nature of that preventative intervention, how to classify response, the nature of the multidisciplinary evaluation prior to special education, and the function and design of special education.

NUMBER OF PREVENTION TIERS

The first decision that schools face is determining the number of prevention tiers that constitute their RTI system. General education is always considered the first tier, and students who are targeted for preventative intervention must first show evidence of failing to respond to this universal core program. Beyond general education, however, RTI systems may include any number of tiers prior to special education. Some RTI systems incorporate general education along with a second tier of prevention. This second tier is more intensive

Figure 1. Sample RTI Model

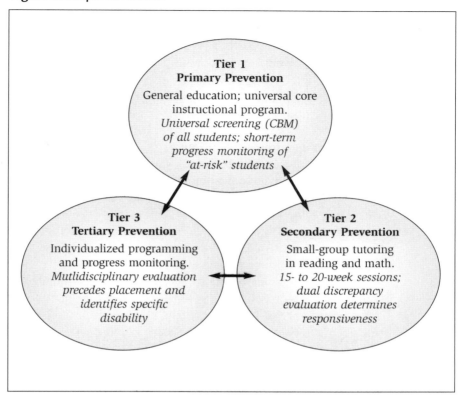

than general education but less intensive than special education, and students must also show poor response to this second tier of prevention before special education is initiated at a third tier. Other RTI systems incorporate additional tiers of prevention to separate general and special education, with special education used as the fourth, fifth, or sixth tier.

Our recommendation is that schools employ three tiers, with only one tier separating general and special education. We make this recommendation because of the difficulty of designing more than one tier of preventative intervention that can be reliably distinguished in format, nature, style, and intensity both from general and from special education. Given this difficulty, extra tiers separating general and special education begin to resemble the intensity of special education. So, adequate response to these extra tiers represents a shaky basis for assuming that a child does not in fact require special education. When considering responsiveness for the purpose of deciding that the child requires special education, prevention should represent a research-validated form of instruction with a format, nature, style, and intensity that can be implemented by practitioners who are more readily available than special educators, including well-trained and supervised paraprofessionals.

IDENTIFYING STUDENTS FOR PREVENTION

Regardless of the number of tiers employed, a second component of RTI with which schools struggle is how students are targeted to receive prevention beyond the universal core program. Some RTI systems employ 1-time universal screening, whereby all children in a school are assessed on a brief measure at the beginning of the school year. Students who score below a norm-referenced cut-point (e.g., < 25th percentile on the Woodcock Reading Mastery Tests – Word Identification) or below a performance benchmark associated with poor long-term outcome (e.g., < 15 on curriculum-based measurement word identification fluency at the beginning of first grade) enter preventative intervention. In systems that rely on 1-time universal screening to identify students who enter preventative intervention, the assumption is that low performance relative to the cut-point or the performance benchmark at the beginning of a school year constitutes evidence that the child has failed to respond to the Tier 1 universal core program during previous school years and therefore requires preventative intervention.

In other versions of RTI, universal screening is conducted to identify a subset of students who are "potentially" at risk for poor outcomes and then the performance of these students is monitored for a relatively short time to (dis)confirm the risk status suggested via universal screening. Only the subset of students who (a) first meet the universal screening cut-point and (b) then show poor rates of improvement over 5 to 8 weeks of Tier 1 general education are deemed in need of a preventative intervention.

We recommend that schools use universal screening in combination with at least 5 weeks of weekly progress monitoring in response to general education to identify students who require preventative intervention. Our rationale is that 1-time universal screening at the beginning of the year may over-identify students who require preventative intervention. In our research conducted in reading at first grade, for example, 50% of students identified on the basis of 1-time universal screening in fact made good progress over the course of first grade without any preventative intervention. Identifying students for preventative intervention based on 1-time universal screening means that schools are pressed to deliver costly prevention to large numbers of students who do not need those services. This means that schools must water down the nature of prevention. By contrast, our research (Compton, Fuchs, Fuchs, & Bryant, 2006) shows that with 5 weeks of weekly progress monitoring in reading, the number of students who are identified for Tier 2, who do not actually need Tier 2, is reduced substantially or even eliminated. Hence, we recommend that schools incorporate short-term progress monitoring in response to general education for identifying which students require preventative intervention.

WHAT PREVENTATIVE INTERVENTION LOOKS LIKE

Two models of preventative intervention are prominent within RTI. The first, called "problem solving," relies on preventative interventions that are individually tailored to meet the student's learning needs. As reflected in the literature, these preventative interventions often conceptualize academic deficiencies as motivation problems. These interventions therefore attempt to increase student performance on skills that are already acquired, rather than designing instruction to develop new skills. Typically, the school psychologist assumes major responsibility, in collaboration with other professionals, for designing the individually-tailored preventative interventions that vary in form and function across students.

A second approach to preventative intervention is to rely on "standard protocols" that have been shown via randomized controlled studies to improve most students' academic achievement. In contrast to the problem-solving approach, the standard treatment protocol typically is designed to promote the acquisition of new skills, while incorporating standard methods for addressing behavioral and attention deficits so that instruction may proceed smoothly. The typical standard treatment protocol is more intensive than Tier 1 general education because it relies on small-group tutoring by a professional teacher or a trained and supervised paraprofessional, 3 to 4 times per week for anywhere from 10 to 20 weeks; because it attempts to ensure mastery for the majority of students; because it minimizes transitions and maintains good pace, while attempting to ensure high levels of on task behavior; and because it incorporates self-regulation strategies to increase goal-oriented behavior. In addition, the tutoring protocols are sometimes scripted; in all cases, highly prescriptive. Therefore, the tutoring sessions can be roughly standardized across tutors and provide the opportunity to estimate the accuracy with which the tutoring protocol is implemented. Reliance on research-validated preventative interventions that have been shown to be highly effective for the majority of students speaks to a fundamental assumption within RTI: If the child responds inadequately to instruction that benefits most students, then the assessment eliminates instructional quality as a viable explanation for poor academic growth and, instead, provides evidence of a disability. This differs from a problem-solving approach where the preventative intervention does not represent "instruction that benefits most students," but instead is an individually tailored program.

We recommend that schools rely on a combination of approaches with a standard treatment protocol used for academic difficulties and a problem-solving approach used for obvious behavioral problems. Our rationale is that standard treatment protocols have been shown to be highly effective for academic deficits; therefore, the quality of preventative intervention does not depend on local professionals who may have uneven training and background in instructional design. In a related way, with a standard treatment protocol, the nature of the preventative intervention to which students do and do not respond is public, clear, and represents "instruction that benefits most students." By contrast, when a problem-solving approach is applied to remedy reading or math difficulties, there is greater responsibility on the RTI system to maintain records about the nature of a student's preventative intervention; there is more parental responsibility to judge whether an individually-tailored preventative intervention is viable; and there is a weaker basis for presuming that inadequate response eliminates poor instruction as the cause for insufficient learning. For these reasons, the problem-solving approach may morph RTI into something that resembles prereferral intervention, whereby schools in the past have relied on idiosyncratic and watered-down interventions, such as moving seats or adding homework, to address serious academic difficulties. Nevertheless, when dramatic behavior difficulties occur in combination with academic deficits, a problem-solving approach should be used to resolve the behavior problem. An academic difficulty that persists despite a well-designed and functional behavioral program then requires a standard treatment protocol to build new academic skills.

CLASSIFYING RESPONSE

To classify response, research provides four options. Two rely on the student's status when the preventative intervention ends. Torgesen et al. (2001) suggested that at the end of intervention, any student whose performance is above the 24th percentile be deemed responsive. The idea is that the intervention has "normalized" the student's performance. A second option, which also relies on final status, employs a criterion-referenced benchmark for determining whether the intervention has made a sufficient impact to ensure long-term success. Good, Simmons, and Kame'enui (2001), for example, suggest administering curriculum-based measurement at the end of intervention, and designating all students who achieve the benchmark as responsive. A third option relies on slope of improvement during preventative intervention, rather than the student's final status at the end of intervention. In this way, Vellutino et al. (1996) suggested rank ordering the slopes of improvement for students who receive preventative intervention. The cut-point for distinguishing response from nonresponse is the median of those rank-ordered slopes. Finally, L. S. Fuchs and Fuchs (1998) combine the use of slope of improvement with final status for classifying response in the following way. To be deemed unresponsive, a student must demonstrate a "dual discrepancy," whereby slope of improvement and final level are both at least 1 standard deviation below that of peers.

We recommend that a dual discrepancy be used to designate unresponsiveness. Final status alone is problematic because it permits some students to be classified as unresponsive despite strong improvement. That is, they begin intervention far below the normalized or benchmark final criterion, and despite strong growth, they remain below the criterion at the end of intervention. Slope of improvement alone is problematic because it permits some students to be classified as unresponsive even though they complete intervention meeting the normalized or benchmark performance criterion. By contrast, a dual discrepancy, which simultaneously considers slope of improvement and final status, permits the unresponsive designation only when a student (a) fails to make adequate growth and (b) completes intervention below the normalized or benchmark criterion. In a recent working meeting on RTI-LD classification (D. Fuchs, Compton, Fuchs, & Davis, in press), dual discrepancy emerged as a tenable approach for designating unresponsiveness. It was adequately sensitive and specific with respect to future low reading performance, even as it identified students with a severe form of reading disability with realistic prevalence rates. Additional work is required to examine how alternative methods for classifying LD within an RTI system perform, but in the meantime, dual discrepancy appears promising.

MULTIDISCIPLINARY EVALUATION

Another issue that schools face in building their RTI model is how to design the multidisciplinary evaluation that federal law requires for special education placement. In some RTI systems, multidisciplinary evaluations are comprehensive, with a standard battery of assessments administered to all students. In other RTI systems, multidisciplinary evaluations are specific to the questions that arise as a function of the student's participation in Tiers 1 and 2. Another dimension along which multidisciplinary evaluations differ is whether the assessment is designed to distinguish among LD, mild mental retardation, speech/language impairment, and emotional behavior disorders as the disability underlying the lack of responsiveness. For this purpose, the following types of assessments are typically included: (a) adaptive behavior and intelligence to distinguish between LD and mild mental retardation, (b) expressive and pragmatic language to help inform distinctions between LD and language impairment, and (c) teacher rating scales, classroom observations, and parent interviews. These distinctions are warranted, of course, only if they provide utility for designing instruction and grouping students productively for instruction. Few, if any, strong studies have been conducted to assess the utility of these designations.

Pending such research findings, we recommend that the instructionally focused multidisciplinary evaluation be designed to answer specific questions that arise during general education instruction and previous rounds of prevention and that the special education multidisciplinary evaluation include a process for distinguishing among the high-incidence disabilities. Our recommendation is based on two assumptions. First, a specifically tailored, instructionally focused multidisciplinary evaluation is more efficient than a full-blown evaluation, even as it is more likely to provide useful information for designing special education programs. The second assumption is that distinctions among the high-incidence disability categories may prove helpful to special educators in formulating sensible grouping structures.

SPECIAL EDUCATION

Most discussions about RTI focus on reforming general education, which is conceptualized as a research-based, multi-tiered system of preventative intervention to prevent LD for students who are otherwise instructional casualties and to identify LD for students for whom poor instruction is eliminated as an explanation for failure. In these discussions, special education is rarely mentioned, except as the final outcome to be avoided. We believe that this is unfortunate because special education is as much in need of reform as is general education. Moreover, students who prove unresponsive to RTI's preventative intervention deserve a revitalized special education tier to address their serious disability. A reformed special education should rely on lower student-teacher ratios, more instructional time, and use of ongoing progress monitoring, such as curriculum-based measurement, for deductively building programs that are shown empirically to address individual student needs, which have proved unresponsive to a research-validated standard treatment protocol. Without such reform, special education's large student caseloads and unfortunate emphasis on paperwork and procedural compliance preclude effectiveness, and the responsibility for producing strong outcomes, in effect, resides entirely on the general education system. If attention on reforming general education were similarly allocated to reforming special education, then special education would represent a valued tier within RTI's multi-tiered intervention system, not a dreaded outcome of a failed general education system.

We recommend that RTI incorporate special education as an important tier that delivers the most intensive instructional programs designed formatively to address individual needs. This reformed special education should be a flexible service, systematically permitting students to move in and out of this tier as the student's needs change in relation to the demands of the general education curriculum. This recommendation is based on a hope that special education can provide a valuable resource for addressing the needs of students with LD—if special education is reformed and deliberately considered and incorporated within RTI's multi-tiered service delivery system.

AN RTI SYSTEM INCORPORATING THESE RECOMMENDED PRACTICES

In this section, we describe what an RTI system, which incorporates our recommendations, might look like at first grade in reading and math. The RTI system we describe is based on research conducted by the National Research Center on Learning Disabilities, sponsored by the Office of Special Education Programs in the U.S. Department of Education. For studies, see Compton, D. Fuchs et al. (2006), D. Fuchs (in press), L. S. Fuchs, et al. (2005), L. S. Fuchs et al. (2007), and Compton, Fuchs, and Fuchs, (submitted).

"Our School" uses a *3-tier system*. Tier 2 separates general education (Tier 1) from special education (Tier 3). Tier 1 general education is deemed "generally effective" for two reasons. First, each quarter, the lead reading

First-Grade Curriculum-Based Measures for RTI

Reading: Curriculum-Based Measurement First-Grade Word Identification Fluency

Testing is conducted individually in a quiet location, and the examiner scores the test at the completion of the session. Each alternate form presents the student with a single-page list of 50 words, randomly sampled from a pool of 100 high-frequency pre-primer, primer, and first-grade words. The student reads words aloud for 1 min; if the student hesitates for 3 sec on a word, the tester directs the student to move on. The score is number of words read correctly. For universal screening, each students reads from two alternate forms in the same session; the screening score is the average of the two scores. For indexing response, the student reads from one alternate form each week (with weekly scores graphed), and at the time when responsiveness is indexed, the student reads again from two alternate forms in the same testing session, with the two scores averaged.

Math: Curriculum-Based Measurement First-Grade Computation

Testing is conducted in whole-class or small-group arrangements and scored later by the tester. Each alternate form is a single page displaying 25 items that systematically represent the problems incorporated in the annual first-grade curriculum. Each alternate form includes different problems in random order, but incorporates the same type of problems in the same proportion. Students have 2 min to complete as many problems as they can. The score is number of digits written correctly (within the answer, not the work). For universal screening, each student completes two alternate forms on two consecutive weeks; the screening score is the average of the two scores. For indexing response, the student completes one alternate form each week (weekly scores are graphed), and at the time when responsiveness is indexed, the student again completes two alternate forms on two consecutive weeks, with the two scores averaged.

---

teacher and the lead math teacher observe each first-grade teacher implementing the universal core instructional program and has documented strong implementation. The second form of evidence for the effectiveness of first-grade Tier 1 reading and math general education programming is based on the school's track records. That is, the previous year's first-grade cohort, on average, demonstrated a strong slope of improvement: in reading, an average increase of 1.8 words per week on curriculum-based measurement word identification fluency (WIF); in math, an average increase of 0.50 digits per week on curriculum-based measurement computation (COMP; see box, "First-Grade Curriculum-Based Measures for RTI"). These figures are commensurate with the weekly rate of improvement for typically-developing students in first grade (1.75 words per week increase in reading; 0.50 digits per week increase in math). Moreover, during the previous year, only 3 of 60 (i.e., 5%) first graders failed to achieve the end-of-year WIF benchmark of 60 words read correctly in 1 min. Only 2 (i.e., 3.3%) failed to achieve the end-of-year COMP benchmark of 18 digits correct in 2 min.

To *target students for prevention,* "Our School" combines universal screening with 5 weeks of short-term progress monitoring. That is, children move on to preventative tutoring only when their universal screening scores are low and when they also demonstrate poor growth in response to the Tier 1 universal program. For universal screening, "Our School" assesses all students in September of first grade in the same test session on two alternate forms of WIF (see box "First-Grade Curriculum-Based Measures for RTI"), averaging performance across the two forms, and assesses all students in September of first grade on two alternate forms of COMP on two consecutive weeks, averaging performance across the two forms. In reading, students whose average WIF screening score is below 15 move on to weekly progress monitoring for 5 weeks. Students whose rate of weekly WIF increase (computed as slope on a line of best fit) is below 1.8 then move on to Tier 2 small-group tutoring. In math, students whose average COMP screening score is below 5 move on to weekly progress monitoring for 5 weeks. Students whose rate of weekly COMP increase (computed as slope on a line of best fit) is below 0.50 then move on to Tier 2 small-group tutoring.

For students who move on to *preventative tutoring* (i.e., Tier 2), "Our School" relies on standard treatment protocols, which are modeled after validated tutoring programs at first grade. In reading, students receive 45 min of instruction four times each week in groups of 3 students for 15 weeks. In math, students receive 30 min of tutoring plus 10 of computerized drill and practice on math facts, three times each week, also in groups of 3 students but for 20 weeks. Across reading and math, tutors are trained paraprofessionals who are observed once each week by the lead reading teacher and receive corrective feedback. Also, once each week, the lead reading teacher meets with all tutors for 1 hr to examine students' progress monitoring graphs (WIF in reading; COMP in math) and to problem solve about difficulties the tutors are experiencing in effecting growth, in managing student behavior, and in keeping groups moving forward when a single student is not keeping pace. In reading, the tutoring sessions focus on phonological awareness, letter-sound recognition, decoding, sight word recognition, and short-story reading, with highly explicit instruction. In math, the tutoring sessions focus on number concepts, numeration, operations, basic fact strategies, story problems, and missing addends. In reading and math, self-regulated learning strategies are incorporated to increase motivation and goal-directed learning.

To *determine whether students have responded to small-group tutoring,* WIF and COMP are again used, in reading and math, respectively. In reading, students whose WIF slope of improvement is less than 1.8 and whose projected year-end WIF score is less than 30 are deemed unresponsive. In math, students whose COMP slope of improvement is less than 0.50 and whose projected year-end WIF score is less than 20 are deemed unresponsive. Students who meet these responsiveness criteria return to the Tier 1 universal program, but weekly progress monitoring continues. That way, if the student fails to maintain adequate growth rates (i.e., a 1.8-word weekly increase on WIF; a 0.50-digit weekly increase on COMP), a Tier 2 program can be re-initiated.

For students who fail to meet the criteria in reading or math, however, an *instructionally focused evaluation* is conducted in consonance with the special education multidisciplinary evaluation. Written parental consent for the multidisciplinary evaluation is obtained. The evaluation is tailored to answer questions that arose during Tier 1 general education and Tier 2 tutoring and to formulate distinctions among LD, mild mental retardation, language impairment, and emotional behavior disorders. For making these distinctions, relatively brief measures are used: the 2-subtest Wechsler Abbreviated Scale of Intelligence and the Vineland Adaptive Rating Scale to identify mental retardation; language tests to identify language impairment; and brief rating scales, classroom observations, and parent interviews to identify emotional behavioral disorders.

At "Our School," *special education* represents a valuable and vital tier in the 3-tier prevention system. Special educators incorporate formative decision making based on ongoing progress monitoring (at first grade, WIF in reading; COMP in math) to design individually-tailored special education programs. The goal is to use the progress monitoring to deductively formulate a program that is effective for the student whose response to the standard treatment protocol (at Tier 2) was poor. The key distinctions between Tiers 2 and 3 are: the special educators rely on lower student-teacher ratios (typically 1:1 or 1:2), provide more instructional time (up to 1.5 hr per day), and systematically use ongoing progress monitoring to deductively formulate individually tailored programs. We also note that "Our School's" Tier 3 special education is a flexible service, permitting exit and reentry as the student's needs change in relation to the demands of the general education curriculum. At first grade, students exit special education when their WIF slope of improvement exceeds 1.8 words increase per week and when their *projected* year-end performance exceeds 50 and/or when their COMP slope of improvement exceeds 0.50 digits increase per week and when their projected year-end performance exceeds 20. When a student exits special education, they return to Tier 2 or Tier 1, as deemed most appropriate by the school staff, and weekly progress monitoring continues. That way, the school knows if the student fails to maintain adequate growth rates and formulates a data-based decision about whether the student needs to move to a more intensive tier within the multi-tier prevention system.

Before closing, we note that although research on the RTI process provides the basis for many strong guidelines for implementation, those guidelines are tentative, because additional promising investigations are underway. As new findings emerge, many of the guidelines and recommendations we have offered in this article will undoubtedly change, with corresponding improvements in the prevention and identification of learning disabilities.

ADDITIONAL RESOURCES

To obtain tutoring manuals based on studies conducted by the National Research Center on Learning Disabilities, contact flora.murray@vanderbilt. edu

REFERENCES

Compton, D. L., Fuchs, D., Fuchs, L. S., & Bryant, J. D. (2006). Selecting at-risk readers in first grade for early intervention: A two-year longitudinal study of decision rules and procedures. *Journal of Educational Psychology, 98*, 394–409.

Compton, D. L., Fuchs, L. S., & Fuchs, D. (submitted). *The course of reading and mathematics development in first grade: Identifying latent trajectories and early predictors.* Manuscript submitted for publication.

Fuchs, D., Compton, D. L., Fuchs, L. S., & Davis, G. C. (in press). Making "secondary intervention" work in a three-tier responsiveness-to-intervention model: Findings from the first-grade longitudinal study at the National Research Center on Learning Disabilities. *Reading and Writing: An Interdisciplinary Journal.*

Fuchs, L. S., Compton, D. L., Fuchs, D., Paulsen, K., Bryant, J. D., & Hamlett, C. L. (2005). The prevention, identification, and cognitive determinants of math difficulty. *Journal of Educational Psychology, 97*, 493–513.

Fuchs, L. S., & Fuchs, D. (1998). Treatment validity: A unifying concept for reconceptualizing the identification of learning disabilities. *Learning Disabilities Research and Practice, 13*(4), 204–219.

Fuchs, L. S., Fuchs, D., Compton, D. L., Bryant, J. D., Hamlett, C. L., & Seethaler, P. M. (2007). Mathematics screening and progress monitoring at first grade: Implications for responsiveness-to-intervention. *Exceptional Children, 73*, 311–330.

Good, R. H. III, Simmons, D. C., & Kame'enui, E. J. (2001). The importance and decision-making utility of a continuum of fluency-based indicators of foundational reading skills for third-grade high-stakes outcomes. *Scientific Studies of Reading, 5*(3), 257–288.

Torgesen, J. K., Alexander, A. W., Wagner, R. K., Rashotte, C. A., Voeller, K. K. S., & Conway, T. (2001). Intensive remedial instruction for children with severe reading disabilities: Immediate and long-term outcomes from two instructional approaches. *Journal of Learning Disabilities*, *34*(1), 33–58.

Vaughn, S. R., & Fuchs, L. S. (2003). Redefining learning disabilities as inadequate response to treatment: Rationale and assumptions. *Learning Disabilities Research and Practice, 18*(3), 137–146.

Vellutino, F., Scanlon, D. M., Sipay, E. R., Small, S. G., Pratt, A., Chen, R., et al. (1996). Cognitive profiles of difficult-to-remediate and readily remediated poor readers: Early intervention as a vehicle for distinguishing between cognitive and experiential deficits as basic cause of specific reading disability. *Journal of Educational Psychology, 88*, 601–638.

This work was supported in part by Grant #H324U010004 from the U.S. Department of Education, Office of Special Education Programs, and Core Grant #HD15052 from the National Institute of Child Health and Human Development to Vanderbilt University. Statements do not reflect the position or policy of these agencies, and no official endorsement by them should be inferred.

Originally published in *TEACHING Exceptional Children,* Vol. 39, No. 5, pp. 14–20.

4

Primary Prevention in Classroom Reading Instruction

Barbara R. Foorman

The Individuals With Disabilities Education Improvement Act of 2004 (IDEA, 2004) contains an enormously important provision—the provision that up to 15% of funds can be used for prevention. The possibility of preventing learning difficulties before they start and of eliminating the need that a student fail before funds for intervention become available are intuitively appealing ideas. Now the challenge is to make prevention at the classroom level successful for all children. The focus in this article is on beginning reading instruction in primary-grade classrooms, with particular attention to (a) evidence-based practices that promote classroom reading success, and (b) the criteria for selecting core reading materials that address the needs of a diverse group of students.

EVIDENCE-BASED PRACTICES IN CLASSROOM READING

Consensus Reports of Crucial Elements

Consensus documents are available that describe the components of effective reading instruction (National Institute of Child Health and Human Development [NICHD], 2000; National Research Council [NRC]), 1998. These components are

- Phonemic awareness and phonemic decoding skills.
- Fluency in word recognition and text processing.

- Construction of meaning.
- Vocabulary.
- Spelling.
- Writing.

These components are the same whether one is discussing classroom reading instruction or instruction for children at risk for reading problems, with the difference being that children at risk for reading disabilities need more explicit and more intense instruction in these elements (Foorman & Torgesen, 2001). Most of these components of effective instruction have been incorporated into the technical assistance for Reading First, the primary-grade portion of No Child Left Behind (NCLB, 2001). However, the language arts components of the crucial elements—vocabulary, spelling, and writing—are neglected in many states' and districts' implementations of Reading First, to the detriment of children's later reading comprehension (Dickinson, McCabe, Anastasop-oulos, Peisner-Feinberg, & Poes, 2003; Mehta, Foorman, Branum-Martin, & Taylor, 2005).

Empirical Investigations of Instructional Practices

Instructional practices exist in a set of nested relations: students nested within classrooms and classrooms nested within schools. At the school level, many researchers have noted characteristics of schools with outstanding achieve-ment (e.g., Bryk & Schneider, 2002; Denton, Foorman, & Mathes, 2003; Hoffman, 1991; Puma et al., 1997; Shavelson & Berliner, 1988; Taylor, Pearson, Clark, & Walpole, 2000; Weber, 1971): positive social climate, strong instruc-tional leadership, increased amount of time available for reading instruction, high expectations and strong accountability, continuous monitoring of student achievement, ongoing professional development based on effective reading strategies, and integral parental involvement. Characteristics of ineffective schools have also been noted. Seven ways in which ineffective schools differed from their demographically matched peers are described by the National Research Council (1998):

> (1) they were not academically focused; (2) the school's daily sched-ule was not an accurate guide to academic time usage; (3) resources often worked at cross-purposes instructionally; (4) principals seemed uninterested in curricula; (5) principals were relatively passive in the recruitment of new teachers, in the selection of professional develop-ment topics and opportunities for the teachers, and in the perform-ance of teacher evaluations; (6) libraries and other media resources were rarely used to their full potential; and (7) few systems of pub-lic reward for students' academic excellence were in place. (p. 130)

At the teacher level, effective classrooms have more time on instructional activities and more engaged students (Fisher et al., 1980; Stallings, 1980);

more small-group instruction; good classroom management; and more active instruction (Anderson, Evertson, & Brophy, 1979). Pressley and others (2001) compared academic engagement and classroom literacy performance for first-grade teachers that were most-effective-for-locale and least-effective-for-locale. Classrooms of effective teachers were characterized by excellent classroom management, balanced teaching of skills, scaffolding and differentiated instruction, cross-curricular connections, and encouragement of student self-regulation. Other researchers have found similar "best practices" (Cunningham & Allington, 1999; Hoffman, 1991; Rosenshine & Furst, 1973; Taylor et al., 2000; Wharton-McDonald, Pressley, & Hampston, 1998). In ineffective schools, Stringfield and Teddlie (1991) found unengaging tasks and failure to cover the district-mandated curriculum. A shortcoming of these descriptions of what effective teachers do is the failure to link "best practices" with student achievement. Similarly, at the student-level, characteristics have typically been discussed with respect to such group characteristics as socioeconomic status (SES), ethnicity, and achievement levels rather than in terms of individual differences in learning and achievement.

Because students are clustered in classrooms and classrooms exist within schools, a desirable design for addressing the effect of instructional practices on student achievement is to nest student within classroom within school. Studies using such designs reveal more variability between classrooms within schools than between schools (Hanushek, Kain, O'Brien, & Rivkin, 2005), particularly in urban compared to rural settings (Foorman, York, Santi, & Francis, in press). This increased variability in urban schools appears at least partly due to the tendency to move children together from one classroom to the next (i.e., tracking), thereby creating a peer effect that is distinct from teacher effects. For example, in a study of 210 schools, Foorman and colleagues (in press) found that students with low fluency scores at the beginning of first grade had higher fluency outcomes at the end of second grade if they were in classrooms in which their peers had high fluency scores. Thus, peers' oral reading fluency rate was an intervention all by itself. This peer effect was not evident for word recognition, however. Instead, students' word reading outcomes at the end of second grade were predicted by an interaction between high ability in this skill at the beginning of first grade and being in high-skill classrooms.

Thus, the notion of "best practices" can be understood as an interaction of teacher effects, peer effects, and student effects. The NCLB definition of teacher quality as certification, licensure, and degrees has not reliably predicted gains in student achievement (Desimone, Smith, & Frisvold, in press; Hanushek, et al., 2005; McCoach, O'Connell, Reis, & Levitt, 2006). Teachers' verbal IQ (Hanushek et al.) and oral language proficiency in English and Spanish (Cirino, Pollard-Durodola, Foorman, Carlson, & Francis, 2007) relate significantly to student achievement gains. Additionally, teacher knowledge tends to be significantly related to gains in student achievement when teachers are provided professional development (Foorman & Moats, 2004;

McCutchen et al., 2002). Several studies by Foorman and colleagues (Foorman, Francis, Fletcher, Schatschneider, & Mehta, 1998; Foorman et al., 2003; and Foorman et al., 2006); and by Connor and colleagues (Connor, Morrison, & Katch, 2004; Connor, Morrison, & Slominski, 2006) indicate that achievement gains are best explained by interactions between child characteristics and instructional practices.

Foorman and others (1998) examined how the degree of explicitness of letter-sound instruction interacted with students' entering skill in phonemic awareness. They investigated the reading development of 285 first- and second-grade students in 66 classrooms in eight Title I schools, using a multilevel analysis. Thirteen of the teachers were part of an unseen comparison group that represented the district's implicit-code standard instruction. The other 53 teachers participated, with high fidelity, in one of three kinds of classroom reading programs, all of which included a language arts emphasis on writing and read-aloud from quality literature: (a) direct instruction in letter-sound correspondences practiced in controlled vocabulary texts (direct code); (b) less direct instruction in sound-spelling patterns embedded in trade books (embedded code); and (c) implicit instruction in the alphabetic code while reading trade books (implicit code). Students receiving direct code instruction improved in word reading at a faster rate and had higher end-of-year scores than students in the implicit code group, and this growth effect was moderated by level of phonemic awareness at the beginning of the year. Phonemic awareness ability at the beginning of the year was expected to be less related to outcome in the direct code group because more explicit instruction in the alphabetic principle is effective in developing phonemic awareness skill in all children, thereby minimizing the impact of the level of this skill that students bring to the classroom in the fall.

Foorman and colleagues (2003) found a similar interaction of child characteristics with instructional strategies in an investigation of 4,872 kindergarteners in 114 classrooms in 32 Title I schools. Reading curricula in these classrooms varied in the degree of teacher choice and in the degree of incorporation of phonemic awareness and phonics but were all guided by ongoing professional development. Basal readers with less teacher choice and more explicit incorporation of phonemic awareness and phonics had less variable teacher-level means in letter knowledge and phonemic awareness at the end of kindergarten and in reading achievement at the end of first grade. In contrast, a basal with more teacher choice and a moderate number of phonemic awareness activities (mostly in the form of letter-sound instruction) had more variable teacher means but more outliers representing high-scoring children at the end of kindergarten and first grade. Thus, direct systematic phonemic awareness and phonics instruction can raise the performance of low-ability kindergarten students but may constrain the growth of students who have already mastered the alphabetic principle.

In a third study, Foorman and others (2006) explored how teacher's allocation of instructional time and their teaching competencies interacted with students' initial ability to predict literacy outcomes, with curriculum differences controlled. Ratings of teaching effectiveness and time allocation were obtained in 107 first- and second-grade classrooms in 17 high-poverty schools. Twenty time allocation variables were reduced into seven patterns of literacy activities that were examined as predictors of reading and spelling outcomes. Students' initial reading ability and interactions of teaching-effectiveness ratings by time-allocation components significantly predicted reading and spelling outcomes. For example, higher rated teachers in both grades had students with higher reading comprehension outcomes, and more highly rated second-grade teachers spent more time on vocabulary. Students' word attack outcomes were higher (a) when teachers spent more time reading books than giving directions or preparing to instruct, and (b) when highly rated first-grade teachers engaged in more phonemic awareness and alphabetic skill instruction and less wasted instructional time. Students with high initial reading ability had lower word-reading and spelling outcomes when their low-rated teachers engaged in more time on grammar, mechanics, and spelling instruction. This final result was explained by observations of poor-quality spelling instruction.

With curricular effects controlled (owing to lack of random assignment), the impact of ratings of teaching effectiveness in these 17 high poverty schools were weak (effect sizes between 1% and 4%) and the impact of initial reading ability was moderately strong (effect sizes between 33% and 50%). In this study, the use of reform curricula (Success for All, Reading Mastery, Open Court, and a revised Houghton Mifflin curriculum), coupled with teacher professional development, worked to reduce variability among teachers and to promote student achievement gains.

The research of Connor and colleagues has also found interactions of child by instruction. Their observational system codes whether the teacher or child is directing the child's attention (i.e., teacher-managed activities and child-managed activities) as well as whether the instruction is code-focused or meaning-focused. In a study of first-grade classrooms, Connor et al. (2004) found that students with lower fall decoding and vocabulary scores exhibited greater decoding growth in classrooms that spent more time on teacher-managed explicit decoding activities, with small amounts of child-managed meaning-focused activities in the fall that increased across the year. However, the opposite occurred for students that started the year with higher decoding and vocabulary scores. For them, time allocated to explicit decoding instruction had little impact, whereas time allocated to child-managed meaning-focused activities throughout the year resulted in greater decoding growth. In a preschool study, Connor et al. (2006) found that time allocated to teacher-managed (and teacher–child-managed) emergent code-focused activities was related to preschoolers' alphabetic and letter-word recognition growth, whereas time allocated to child-managed meaning-focused activities (e.g., book reading) was related to vocabulary growth.

In summary, the studies by Foorman and Connor and colleagues show that "best practices" in primary-grade classrooms are complex interactions of school-level, teacher-level, and student-level effects. Schools reside in urban or rural settings and vary in their access to social and economic capital. Characteristics of principals and teachers vary as they relate to instructional knowledge and skill. Curriculum varies in the degree to which it is scripted and explicit. Teachers' implementation of the curriculum varies in its fidelity as well as its adaptation to the students' entering abilities and changing skill trajectories. The question to ask about beginning reading instruction, then, is not "What are best practices?" but rather "What instructional activities are appropriate for this student at this phase of his or her reading development to maximize achievement outcomes?" In academically diverse classrooms, teachers will need to become expert in assessing students' entering literacy levels, differentiating instruction in small groups on the basis of that assessment, and reshuffling group membership on the basis of continual monitoring of student progress. Only in this way will teachers be able to prevent instructional causalities in the general education classroom.

CRITERIA FOR SELECTING CORE READING MATERIALS FOR DIVERSE CLASSROOMS

What Is a Core Reading Program?

For the first 200 years of American history, the selection of text for reading instruction was simple: The Lord's Prayer and the Bible. Reading was taught by the ABC method, whereby words were spelled before they were pronounced. Later, with the introduction of such spelling books as *Noah Webster's Blue Back Speller,* words were divided into syllables. The advent of reading series began in 1936 with the *McGuffey Eclectic Readers.* These readers dominated reading instruction for 60 years and combined phonics and whole-word approaches. From the 1920s to 1960, the whole-word, or "look-say," method dominated the reading series and the famous Scott Foresman "Dick, Jane, Sally, and Spot" was considered the dominant reading series of the time. From the 1960s to the current day, the reading series have shifted from those with a predominantly phonics emphasis to those with a predominantly meaning or literature-based emphasis every twenty years or so. These beginning reading series have come to be called *basal reading programs* because they serve as the "base" for reading instruction. More recently, educators have referred to basal reading programs as the core reading program to distinguish them from intervention programs for struggling readers.

Guides to Evaluating Core Reading Programs

In 2000 the alphabetic subgroup of the National Reading Panel (NRP; NICHD, 2000) concluded their meta-analysis of the impact of phonemic awareness and phonics programs on beginning reading outcomes with the statement that systematic instruction in phonemic awareness and phonics enhanced children's success in learning to read (see also Ehri, Nunes, Willows, Schuster, Yaghoub-Zadeh, & Shanahan, 2001; Ehri, Nunes, Stahl, & Willows, 2001). Those results from the NRP and results from the vocabulary, reading fluency, and comprehension subgroup of the NRP were incorporated into the implementation of the Reading First component of NCLB. The Reading First legislation emphasized the importance of using scientifically based reading research for making instructional decisions by using this term over 100 times. The term "scientifically based reading research" quickly achieved acronym status (i.e., SBRR).

In support of the SBRR requirement, the U.S. Department of Education sponsors a Web site called the What Works Clearinghouse (www.whatworks.ed.gov) that features evidence-based studies of the effects of curriculum on students' achievement outcomes. The U.S. Department of Education also funds technical assistance centers in Oregon, Texas, and Florida to help states, districts, and schools implement the requirements of Reading First. Simmons and Kame'enui (2003) at the Oregon Center produced a document in 2002 called "A Consumer's Guide to Evaluating a Core Reading Program Grades K–3: A Critical Elements Analysis." This document was used by states and districts as a checklist for selecting reading instructional materials in Reading First schools. The Florida Center created a scoring rubric and rated the six core reading programs that were on the State of Florida's reading adoption list (Al Otaiba, Kosanovich-Grek, Torgesen, Hassler, & Wahl, 2005).

The Oregon Center's Consumer's Guide suggests that educators select a core reading program by first considering (a) evidence of efficacy established through rigorously designed experimental studies, and (b) relevance to the demographic characteristics of the students who will use the program. At a second stage, the Guide includes an analysis of crucial analyses to help educators determine whether the five major components of reading instruction emphasized by the NRP are adequately addressed: phonemic awareness, phonics, fluency, vocabulary, and reading comprehension. Educators are recommended to review elements (a) in terms of the program's scope and sequence, (b) within a lesson or series of 2 to 3 successive lessons, and (c) across a series of 10 consecutive lessons (to analyze a "skill trace"). Elements are to be rated as (a) not satisfactorily meeting the criterion, (b) partially meeting or exceeding the criterion, or (c) consistently meeting or exceeding the criterion.

The Florida Center's rubric consists of the following categories:

1. Are all five components from the NRP present and prominent?
2. Is instruction within each component explicit and systematic?
3. Is the sequence for instruction organized sequentially?
4. Is student material coordinated with the teacher's guide?
5. Is instruction across components clearly linked?

Staff members from the Florida Center, who were highly knowledgeable in reading content and pedagogy, independently rated the six basal programs under consideration for adoption in Florida during 2002 to 2003 according to the presence (yes/no) and quality (acceptable/not acceptable) of these five categories. Interrater reliability was 100%. Reviewers also noted how the program aligned with SBRR. Al Otaiba and colleagues (2005) found that core reading programs aligned with Reading First shared common features: (a) a clearly articulated statement of SBRR, (b) explicit instructional strategies, and (c) consistent organizational and instructional routines.

Determining Pedagogical Adequacy of Core Reading Programs

By asking educators to rate essential elements within and across lessons, Oregon's Consumer Guide and Florida's rubrics prompt educators to consider whether core reading programs are based on sound principles of learning. That step is crucial in deciding whether a core program will provide the right pedagogical content for a diverse classroom of students. Simply put, teachers need to ask whether the content of the teacher's guide is research based and clearly organized and whether the text in the pupil edition allows their students sufficient practice to master the instructional strategies covered in the lessons.

Several researchers have developed techniques for quantifying the information in the teacher's and pupil editions (Foorman, Francis, Davidson, Harm, & Griffin, 2004; Hiebert, 2002; Stein, Johnson, & Gutlohn, 1999). Hiebert's model uses the percentage of words within a text that come from different word-frequency zones and that have particular vowel patterns to establish text difficulty. Stein and colleagues analyzed sound-spelling patterns of the text in the pupil edition and phonics support materials from the first half of first grade from seven basal series submitted for 1996 California adoption. On the basis of instructional strategies presented in each lesson, words in the text selections were categorized as Dolch List sight words (Dolch, 1948), story sight words, wholly decodable words, and nondecodable and noninstructed words. Only one of the seven basal series had a majority of words (i.e., 52%) that were wholly decodable. When the percentage of sight words (i.e., Dolch List and story words; 46%) was added, this program yielded a 98% accuracy rate, which meant that 98% of the words could be correctly identified given the instructional strategies provided in the lessons in the teacher's edition. In the other six programs, the words in the text selections were primarily sight words (34%–60%), with less than 15% wholly decodable. Accuracy rates ranged from 43% to 68% in those programs, assuming students actually learned the sight words. Stein and others also analyzed decodability in the phonics readers and found the percentage of wholly decodable words to be somewhat higher in those six programs (32%–50%). These percentages were similar to those found by Beck and McCaslin (1978) in their analysis of meaning-emphasis basal programs from the 1970s.

Foorman and colleagues (2004) developed a relational database to analyze the lexical, semantic, and syntactic variability in the text selections used in six basal reading programs published between 1995 and 2000. Like Stein and others (1999), they examined the letter-sound correspondences and sight words taught and their connection with the text selections. Unlike Stein and others, however, Foorman and colleagues computed decodability based on *consistency* of sound-spelling relations rather than simply *regularity* of spelling patterns. For example, the vowel team *ai* might have been taught only as the "long a" sound as in *maid.* If so, then the word said would be counted as nondecodable when presented unless it was taught holistically as a sight word. Another example is multisyllabic words. Counting as decodable the untaught, inconsistent variants of multisyllabic spelling patterns (e.g., silent letters as in *answer,* vowel insertions as in *wasn't,* or consonant doubling as in *happy*) would lead to inflated decodability and accuracy rates.

Foorman and colleagues (2004) also went beyond the phonics analysis of Stein and others and analyzed the semantic and syntactic features of text selections by analyzing words in the texts for their oral and printed vocabulary levels and by calculating the percentage of sentences with embedded clauses and prepositional phrases. The vocabulary demands of all but one of the programs were well above the oral and printed vocabulary of most first graders, giving teachers an opportunity to expand students' oral vocabulary (but possibly confounding an emphasis on decoding instruction). Another program stood out compared with the others in the linguistic complexity of its sentences.

Adoptions in Texas and in California tend to determine the content of basal reading programs across the country because one fifth of the nation's public school students live in those two states. The 2000 and 2002 adoptions in those states mandated 75% to 80% decodable texts for first-grade reading programs. Only one program in the Foorman and others' (2004) analysis met that mandate at the type (unique words) and token (repetition of words) level. Another program met the mandate at the token level. This latter program also provided the highest accuracy rate at first and last presentation of word types (62.16% and 75.97%, respectively). Teaching a phonics strategy at the *first* presentation of a word would seem highly desirable. Also, repeating the word more than once would seem advantageous. Yet Foorman and colleagues (2004) found that 70% of the words students encountered in text were nondecodable singletons, with only 20% repeated two to five times. Little research exists on the number of repetitions of a word needed to master its recognition. Reitsma (1983) found that four to six repetitions of relatively unfamiliar words was sufficient to increase the speed of word recognition a few days later, but his students were already readers.

Foorman and colleagues (2004) found that the relatively high decodability rate at the token level for several of the basal reading programs was achieved by teaching one third of the words holistically. Holistic instructional strategies are used with high-frequency (e.g., *great*) and irregular (e.g., *yacht*) words and with difficult words added to make text selections more interesting (e.g., *hippopotamus*). This strategy of using holistically taught words to boost accuracy rates and heighten interest has the obvious drawback of increasing demands on memory.

Thus, Foorman and colleagues' (2004) analysis of the lexical, semantic, and syntactic features of six first-grade basal reading programs shows great variability in the approach taken to achieve decodability and the extent to which text selections could be expected to yield accurate phonological recoding of words. This finding is consistent with Juel and Roper/Schneider's (1985) conclusion that "[t]he types of words which appear in beginning reading texts may well exert a more powerful influence in shaping children's word identification strategies than the method of reading instruction" (p. 151). To help educators evaluate the appropriateness of a core reading program for a particular classroom of diverse learners, publishers should be required to reinstate the scope, sequence, and cumulative vocabulary list (with oral and printed word frequency noted, as well as the location of the word in the lessons). Explanations of how phonological-orthographic inconsistencies are handled need to be provided (e.g., fox-box vs. frog-cost; past tense and plurals), as well as multisyllabic parsing strategies. State adoption committees could also require electronic files that would allow the computation of decodability and the number of repetitions of holistically taught words. Such information would help educators decide whether the core reading program provides the pedagogically sound content needed if classroom instruction is to meet the needs of diverse learners and prevent reading difficulties.

CONCLUSION

The provision of up to 15% of IDEA funds to be used for prevention of reading difficulties allows educators an enormous opportunity to enhance general education classroom reading instruction. Research exists that shows the complex interactions of students by instructional strategies that promote reading success within diverse classrooms. This research indicates that "best practices" need to be differentiated to meet the needs of individual students at particular phases of reading development. Rubrics and guides exist to help educators select core reading programs that are research based and well organized. Analyses of the lexical, semantic, and syntactic variables in the text selections of the core reading programs indicate, however, that the research on reading instruction has not necessarily penetrated the pedagogical design of core reading programs, and that no research exists to answer such important questions as "How many repetitions of a word are needed to ensure mastery?" or "What are the appropriate trade-offs between oral and printed vocabulary demands in text?" But the fact that we recognize the importance of asking such questions shows that the science of reading is permeating the instructional core of primary-grade classrooms, an essential step if teachers are to have the materials needed to differentiate instruction to meet the needs of diverse learners and prevent reading failure.

REFERENCES

Al Otaiba, S., Kosanovich-Grek, M. L., Torgesen, J. K., Hassler, L., & Wahl, M. (2005). Reviewing core kindergarten and first-grade reading programs in light of No Child Left Behind: An exploratory study. *Reading and Writing Quarterly, 21*(4), 377–400.

Anderson, L., Evertson, C., & Brophy, J. (1979). An experimental study of effective teaching in first-grade reading groups. *Elementary School Journal, 79,* 193–223.

Beck, I., & McCaslin, E. S. (1978). *An analysis of dimensions that affect the development of code-breaking ability in eight beginning reading programs* (LRDC Rep. No. 1978/6). Pittsburgh, PA: University of Pittsburgh, Learning Research and Development Center.

Bryk, A. S., & Schneider, B. (2002). *Trust in schools: A core resource for improvement.* New York: Russell Sage.

Cirino, P., Pollard-Durodola, S. D., Foorman, B. R., Carlson, C. D., & Francis, D. J. (March, 2007). Teacher characteristics, classroom instruction, and student literacy and language outcomes in bilingual kindergarteners. *Elementary School Journal, 107*(4), 341–364.

Connor, C. M., Morrison, F. J., & Katch, L. E. (2004). Beyond the reading wars: Exploring the effect of child-instruction interactions on growth in early reading. *Scientific Studies of Reading, 8*(4), 305–336.

Connor, C. M., Morrison, F. J., & Slominski, L. (2006). Preschool instruction and children's emergent literacy growth. *Journal of Educational Psychology, 98*(4), 665–689.

Cunningham, P. M., & Allington, R. I. (1999). *Classrooms that work: They can all read and write* (2nd ed.). New York: Longman.

Denton, C., Foorman, B., & Mathes, P. (2003). Schools that 'beat the odds': Implications for reading instruction. *Remedial and Special Education, 24,* 258–261.

Desimone, L., Smith, T., & Frisvold, D. (in press). Teacher quality, evidence-based practice, and students in poverty. In A. Gamoran (Ed.), *Will "No Child Left Behind" help close the poverty gap?* Washington, DC: Brookings Institute.

Dickinson, D. K., McCabe, A., Anastasopoulos, L., Peisner-Feinberg, E. S., & Poes, M. D. (2003). The comprehensive language approach to early literacy: The interrelationships among vocabulary, phonological sensitivity, and print knowledge among preschool-aged children. *Journal of Educational Psychology, 95*(3), 465–481.

Dolch, E. W. (1948). *Problems in reading.* Champaign, IL: Garrard.

Ehri, L., Nunes, S., Willows, D., Schuster, B. V., Yaghoub-Zadeh, Z., & Shanahan, T. (2001). Phonemic awareness instruction helps children read: Evidence from the National Reading Panel's meta-analysis. *Reading Research Quarterly, 36*(3), 250–287.

Ehri L., Nunes, S., Stahl, S., & Willows, D. (2001). Systematic phonics instruction helps students learn to read: Evidence from the National Reading Panel's meta-analysis. *Review of Educational Research, 71*(3), 393–447.

Fisher, C., Berliner, D., Filby, N., Marliave, R., Cahen, L., & Dishaw, M. (1980). Teaching behaviors, academic learning time and student achievement: An overview. In C. Denham & A. Lieberman (Eds.), *Time to learn* (pp. 7–32). Washington, DC: National Institute of Education.

Foorman, B. R., Chen, D. T., Carlson, C., Moats, L., Francis, D. J., & Fletcher, J. (2003). The necessity of the alphabetic principle to phonemic awareness instruction. *Reading and Writing, 16,* 289–324.

Foorman, B. R., Francis, D. J., Davidson, K. C., Harm, M., & Griffin, J. (2004). Variability in text features in six grade 1 basal reading programs. *Scientific Studies of Reading, 82*(2), 167–197.

Foorman, B. R., Francis, D. J., Fletcher, J. M., Schatschneider, C., & Mehta, P. (1998). The role of instruction in learning to read: Preventing reading failure in at-risk children. *Journal of Educational Psychology, 90,* 37–55. [Reprinted in *Major themes in education.* D. Wray (Ed.), (2004), London: Routledge.]

Foorman, B. R., & Moats, L. C. (2004). Conditions for sustaining research-based practices in early reading instruction. *Remedial and Special Education, 25*(1), 51–60.

Foorman, B. R., Schatschneider, C., Eakin, M. N., Fletcher, J. M., Moats, L. C., & Francis, D. J. (2006). The impact of instructional practices in grades 1 and 2 on reading and spelling achievement in high poverty schools. *Contemporary Educational Psychology, 31,* 1–29.

Foorman, B. R., & Torgesen, J. K. (2001). Critical elements of classroom and small-group instruction promote reading success in all children. *Learning Disabilities Research and Practice, 16*(4), 202–211.

Foorman, B. R., York, M., Santi, K. L., & Francis, D. J. (in press). Contextual effects on predicting risk for reading difficulties in first and second grade. *Reading and Writing.*

Hanushek, E. A., Kain, J. F., O'Brien, D. M., & Rivkin, S. G. (2005). *The market for teacher quality.* (Working paper 11154). Cambridge, MA: National Bureau of Economic Research.

Hiebert, E. H. (2002). Standards, assessment, and text difficulty. In A. E. Farstrup & S. J. Samuels (Eds.), *What research has to say about reading instruction* (3rd ed., pp. 337–369). Newark, DE: International Reading Association.

Hoffman, J. V. (1991). Teacher and school effects in learning to read. In R. Barr, M. L. Kamil, P. B. Mosenthal, & P. D. Pearson (Eds.), *Handbook of reading research* (Vol. 2, pp. 911–950). New York: Longman.

Individuals With Disabilities Education Improvement Act of 2004 (IDEA), Pub. L. No. 108-446, 118 Stat 2647-2808, (2004).

Juel, C., & Roper/Schneider, D. (1985). The influence of basal readers on first-grade reading. *Reading Research Quarterly, 20,* 134–152.

McCoach, D. B., O'Connell, A. A., Reis, S. M., & Levitt, H. A. (2006). Growing readers: A hierarchical linear model of children's reading growth during the first 2 years of school. *Journal of Educational Psychology, 98*(1), 14–28.

McCutchen, D., Abbott, R. D., Green, L. B., Beretvas, S. N., Cox, S., Potter, N. S., et al. (2002). Beginning literacy: Links among teacher knowledge, teacher practice, and student learning. *Journal of Learning Disabilities, 35,* 69–86.

Mehta, P. D., Foorman, B. R., Branum-Martin, L., & Taylor, W. P. (2005). Literacy as a unidimensional multilevel construct: Validation, sources of influence, and implications in a longitudinal study in grades 1 to 4. *Scientific Studies of Reading, 9*(2), 85–116.

National Institute of Child Health and Human Development (NICHD). (2000). National Reading Panel–Teaching children to read: Reports of the subgroups (NIH Pub. No. 00-4754). Washington, DC: U.S. Department of Health and Human Services.

National Research Council. (1998). *Preventing reading difficulties in young children. Committee on the Prevention of Reading Difficulties in Young Children, Com-*

mission on Behavioral and Social Science and Education, C. E. Snow, M. S. Burns, and P. Griffin (Eds.). Washington, DC: National Academy Press.

No Child Left Behind Act of 2001, Pub. L. No. 107-110, (2001).

Pressley, M., Wharton-McDonald, R., Allington, R., Block, C. C., Morrow, L., Tracey, D., et al. (2001). A study of effective first grade literacy instruction. *Scientific Studies of Reading, 15*(1), 35–58.

Puma, M. J., Darweit, N., Price, C., Ricciuti, A., Thompson, W., & Vaden-Kiernan, M. (1997). *Prospects: Final report on student outcomes.* Washington, DC: U.S. Department of Education, Planning and Evaluating Service.

Reitsma, P. (1983). Printed word learning in beginning readers. *Journal of Experimental Child Psychology, 36,* 321–339.

Rosenshine, B., & Furst, N. (1973). The use of direct observation to study teaching. In R.M.W. Travers (Ed.), *Second handbook of research on teaching* (pp. 122–183). Chicago: Rand McNally.

Shavelson, R. J., & Berliner, D. C. (1988). Evasion of the education research infrastructure: A reply to Finn. *Educational Researcher, 17,* 9–11.

Simmons, D. C., & Kame'enui, E. J. (2003). *A consumer's guide to evaluating a core reading program grades K–3: A critical elements analysis.* Retrieved December 19, 2006, from http://iris.peabody.vanderbilt.edu/rti03_reading/cons_guide_instr.pdf

Stallings, J. A. (1980). Allocated academic reading time revisited, or beyond time on task. *Educational Researcher, 9,* 11–16.

Stein, M., Johnson, B., & Gutlohn, L. (1999). Analyzing beginning reading programs: The relationship between decoding instruction and text. *Remedial and Special Education, 20,* 275–287.

Stringfield, S., & Teddlie, C. (1991). Observers as predictors of schools' multi-year outlier status. *Elementary School Journal, 9,* 357–376.

Taylor, B. M., Pearson, P. D., Clark, K., & Walpole, S. (2000). Effective schools and accomplished teachers: Lessons about primary-grade reading instruction in low income schools. *Elementary School Journal, 101*(2), 121–165.

Weber, G. (1971). *Inner-city children can be taught to read: Four successful schools* (CGE Occasional Paper No. 18). Washington, DC: Council for Basic Education. (ERIC Document Reproduction Service No. ED 057 125)

Wharton-McDonald, R., Pressley, M., & Hampston, J. M. (1998). Literacy instruction in nine first-grade classrooms: Teacher characteristics and student achievement. *Elementary School Journal, 99,* 101–128.

This work was supported by Grant R305W020001, "Scaling Up Assessment-Driven Intervention Using the Internet and Handheld Computers," from the Institute of Education Sciences in the U.S. Department of Education.

Originally published in *TEACHING Exceptional Children,* Vol. 39, No. 5, pp. 24–30.

5

Children at Risk for Reading Failure: Constructing an Early Screening Measure

G. Nicole Davis, Endia J. Lindo, and Donald L. Compton

With the recent reauthorization of the Individuals With Disabilities Education Improvement Act (IDEA, 2004), states now have the option of discontinuing use of IQ–achievement discrepancy procedures as part of the learning disability (LD) identification process in favor of a Response to Intervention (RTI) approach. RTI is based on the premise that students are identified as LD when their response to an effective educational intervention is dramatically inferior to that of peers (e.g., D. Fuchs, Mock, Morgan, & Young, 2003; Vaughn & Fuchs, 2003). RTI approaches for identifying children with reading disabilities (RD) have advantages over traditional IQ–achievement discrepancy procedures, including earlier identification of RD to avoid a "wait-to-fail" model, a strong focus on providing effective instruction and improving student outcomes, and a decision-making process supported by continuous progress monitoring of skills closely aligned with desired instructional outcomes (see Vaughn & Fuchs).

Schools can operationalize RTI through various methods (see D. Fuchs et al., 2003); current models favor a three-tier system (see Bradley, Danielson, & Hallahan, 2002). In Tier 1, all students participate in generally effective reading instruction in the general education classroom, and the school monitors each student's rate of reading growth. Children whose level of performance and/or rate of improvement are dramatically below that of peers (based on classroom, school, district, state, or national norms) are designated as "at risk"

41

for poor reading outcomes, and possibly RD. Such children move to the second tier in the RTI process.

In Tier 2, students receive small-group instruction and their progress is again monitored. The purpose of this second tier is twofold: to prevent reading difficulty by delivering a more intensive (and presumably effective) intervention that accelerates reading development, and to assess the child's responsiveness to instructional intensity from which the vast majority of children should profit. In the event the child responds, he is returned to classroom instruction and is deemed disability-free. Otherwise, it is assumed that the child has an intrinsic deficit, that is, a putative deficit or disability that prevents the child from benefiting from the instruction (Vaughn & Fuchs, 2003). Failure to respond appropriately to Tier 2 instruction signals a need for the child to move to a third and final RTI tier, synonymous with special education placement, after an abbreviated special education evaluation.

RTI MODELS FOR RD IDENTIFICATION

RTI models for identifying RD rely on accurately identifying children who without Tier 2 tutoring would develop RD. Tier 2 is intended to prevent reading difficulty by delivering a more intensive intervention that accelerates reading development, and to assess the child's responsiveness to this instructional intensity. The success of RTI—in terms of both prevention and identification—hinges on using a diagnostic screening device to accurately determine a "risk pool" of children who require Tier 2 intervention.

By definition, a *diagnostic screening measure* is a brief assessment that provides predictive information about a child's development in a specific academic area. Its purpose is to identify any children who are at risk so that these children can receive extra support through Tier 2 intervention services. This diagnostic screening represents a form of high-stakes decision making—IDEA requires that states identify, locate, and evaluate all children with disabilities (from birth to age 21) who are in need of early intervention or special education services. Given this requirement, RTI procedures for determining RD risk must yield a high percentage of "true positives" (approaching 100%), while at the same time identifying a manageable risk pool by limiting the number of children falsely identified as at risk for RD.

How can practitioners improve their ability to systematically identify children truly in need of Tier 2 intervention, within an RTI model of identification and prevention? The RTI process includes making diagnostic decisions, adapting screening measures as a function of reading development, and continually improving the accuracy of screening decisions. Our recommendations include diversifying screening information to include family risk factors, focusing on first-grade children, and conducting short-term progress monitoring to gauge response to the general education curriculum.

DIAGNOSTIC DECISION MAKING

The majority of RTI models for preventing and identifying children with RD begin with a universal screening device. The school administers this screening measure to all children to identify an initial pool of children suspected of being at risk for developing RD. This risk pool can be further refined by administering additional tests to children whose scores do not clearly distinguish them as at risk for RD. Screening information must then be dichotomized into a yes-no decision of risk for each child screened. In making a diagnostic decision there are four possible outcomes, two that are correct and two that are incorrect:

- In one correct outcome, RD risk is present (or positive); this outcome is referred to as a "true positive." In the other correct outcome, RD risk is absent or negative; this outcome is designated a "true negative."

- Of the two incorrect outcomes, one is "false positive" and the other "false negative." False positives occur when children who eventually become good readers score below the cut score on the screening instrument and are falsely identified as at risk. False positives undermine the intent of RTI by increasing the number of children identified as at risk, and, as a result, stress school resources to provide intervention to an inflated percentage of the population (Fletcher et al., 2002; Jenkins & O'Connor, 2002). False negatives refer to children who score above the cut score on a screening instrument but who later exhibit reading problems. As a result, at-risk children are deprived of the early intervention they require.

Typically, schools make these risk decisions by selecting a critical cut-point of scores. A child scoring below the cut-point is considered at risk of developing RD. The cut-point can be adjusted up or down to produce more or fewer positive decisions. Adjusting the cut-point to be more lenient will increase the probability that a greater percentage of true positives will be identified as at risk for RD. Unfortunately, more lenient cut-points also result in a greater number of false positives. Alternatively, if the cut-point is made stricter to decrease the probability of false positives, then the number of true positives will correspondingly go down. When setting cut-points, schools need to establish a balance between true positives and false positives. This balance should be determined by the negative ramifications of misdiagnosing true positives as not at risk for RD versus the cost of providing Tier 2 intervention to children who are false positives and would develop normally in reading without the intervention.

The vast majority of prediction studies have focused on identifying children at risk of RD prior to the onset of formal reading instruction. Early identification of a risk pool of children facilitates their participation in second-tier intervention before the onset of significant reading problems, and increases the possibility that they will establish and maintain normal levels of growth in critical early reading skills. However, predicting which children are at risk for developing RD based on measures of early language ability and print knowledge has proven problematic. Many kindergarten studies using measures of phonological processing, alphabetic knowledge, general language ability, and print concepts overpredicted risk status with estimates of false positives ranging from 20% to 60% (see Jenkins & O'Connor, 2002; Torgesen, 2002). At the same time, rates of false negatives also have been high, ranging from 10% to 50% (Torgesen). Thus, there is considerable need to improve our ability to identify initial risk within an RTI approach to preventing and identifying RD.

SCREENING WITH AN EYE ON READING DEVELOPMENT

The majority of early reading screeners focus on language-based tasks that are pivotal to the proper development of two broad areas: word reading and language comprehension (Gough & Tunmer, 1986). These two areas interact during reading, but they can also function independently and compete with each other for resources. Jenkins and O'Connor (2002) argued that specific traits that forecast later reading success may vary according to children's reading development, suggesting that the measures included on a screening battery should change as a function of grade level. During early reading development, as children learn to "crack the code," the processes that support word reading ability account for the majority of performance variability on reading tasks. As children become more fluent in recognizing words, the relative importance of word reading in accounting for reading skill variation diminishes and language comprehension skill and background knowledge account for the lion's share of individual differences in reading skill. Although word reading and comprehension skill share many important underlying processes, there are processes unique to each skill. In assessments intended to identify children at risk for future reading problems, it is essential to include predictors sensitive to future word reading and comprehension skills in the screening battery.

COMPONENTS OF WORD READING

Research indicates that phonological awareness skills and emergent print knowledge are the strongest early predictors of word reading development (e.g., Adams, 1990; Scarborough, 1998). Phonological awareness is the explicit knowledge of, and sensitivity to, speech sound segments used in a language. *Phonological awareness* skills facilitate the acquisition of spelling-to-sound translation routines that form the basis of early decoding skill development, and therefore are strongly associated with the development of early word reading skills. Phonological awareness has typically been assessed using a variety of tasks such as rhyming, alliteration, blending of syllables, blending of speech sounds, segmenting of syllables, segmenting of speech sounds, and finally manipulation of syllables and of speech sounds. When choosing among so many different phonological awareness tasks, it is important to make sure that the task used on a screening measure is age appropriate. Schatschneider, Francis, Foorman, Fletcher, and Mehta (1999) reported that blending tasks are more accurate determinants of phonological awareness skills in younger children, whereas deletion tasks are better predictors in older children.

Measures of *emerging print knowledge* have been shown to be strong predictors of early word reading ability. One of the best print knowledge predictors of future word reading skill is letter-naming skill. Letter-name knowledge influences early word reading by promoting the emergence of a phonologically based strategy. This strategy bridges the gap from a strictly visual-cue strategy of word reading to a phonetic-cue strategy. In fact, letter knowledge is a good early predictor of children at risk for future word reading problems independent of phonological awareness skill. When measured in preschool through early first grade, letter knowledge is the single best predictor of subsequent word reading ability (Share, Jorm, Maclean, & Matthews, 2002). Treiman, Weatherston, and Berch (1994) found that children learned letters with the letter sound in their name faster than letters that did not have the letter sound in the name. (For example, children's knowledge of letters such as *v* and *k* was better than *h* and *w*.) With the exception of children with persistent reading problems, who often experience lasting problems retaining short vowel sounds, the predictive utility of letter knowledge quickly diminishes as children learn to read.

In addition to phonological awareness skill and letter knowledge, the amount of time that a child is exposed to print is also important to reading development. As children interact with our writing system they are exposed to the various relationships that constitute our spelling system, and develop an understanding of the basic properties of our writing system. Children as early as first grade become sensitive to letter sequence constraints within the English spelling system (Treiman, 1993). For instance, when first-grade children are asked to choose which letter string (*beff* vs. *ffeb*) looks more like a word they consistently select *beff* over *ffeb*. Kindergarteners, however, do not consistently choose either pair above the level of chance, which means they likely guess; results suggest that performance on this task was related to word reading ability and not age (Compton, 2000). This mental collection of spelling patterns in a language—*orthographic knowledge*—is a necessary part of the ability to identify words rapidly in a text. However, this type of orthographic knowledge is used best as an early predictor to distinguish at-risk children from typically developing children. It loses its predictive power soon after children begin formal reading instruction.

There is some consensus that measures assessing phonological awareness, letter knowledge, print concepts, and orthographic knowledge are particularly sensitive in predicting early word reading problems (Torgesen, 2002). This set of measures is sufficient for kindergarten screening batteries. As children move into first grade, however, screening batteries should broaden to include additional measures assessing decoding and word identification skills.

In the early elementary grades, measures of speeded word recognition emerge as one of the most reliable indicators of serious reading problems (Compton & Carlisle, 1994). Automatic and fluent word recognition is important to comprehension of a text. A child who struggles to recognize words automatically and fluently will have fewer resources available for building meaning out of the text.

COMPONENTS OF READING COMPREHENSION

Reading comprehension relies on more than just accurate and fluent word recognition. Ultimately, the efficiency with which a person builds a mental representation of a text's meaning requires sufficient knowledge of and ability to access vocabulary, grammar, and relevant background knowledge. It comes as no surprise, then, that measures of naming and processing speed, working memory, and oral language improve the prediction of reading comprehension performance. In particular, vocabulary, grammatical ability, and sentence repetition skill have a strong influence on later comprehension even after accounting for participants' age, gender, IQ, and socioeconomic standing.

Vocabulary is the main oral language contributor to word-level comprehension. It supports comprehension because children must be able to efficiently retrieve the meaning of the words in a text. Early vocabulary knowledge has consistently been shown to relate to later reading comprehension skill (see McCardle, Scarborough, & Catts, 2001). Vocabulary is clearly an important variable when predicting long-term reading development and reading disability and can be included in screening batteries as early as preschool (Scarborough, 1991).

At a sentence level, the *grammatical structure* of the language is equally important for construction of text meaning as vocabulary. Grammar comprises both syntax and morphology. Syntax is the rule system within a language that governs the way that words can be arranged within a clause and/or a sentence. Morphology is the smallest unit of meaning contained within a word and is often associated with root words and a combination of prefixes and suffixes to form words. Although less studied than phonological awareness or vocabulary, children's grammatical development in these two areas are good predictors of early reading achievement (Elbro & Scarborough, 2004). Grammatical abilities at the beginning of kindergarten are predictive of variance in reading at the end of first grade (Share, Jorm, Maclean, & Matthews, 1984). Both receptive grammar tasks (such as understanding the meaning of complex syntactic and morphological clauses) and expressive grammar tasks (mean length of utterance and sentence repetition tasks) measured in young children have been shown to account for variance in reading development (Scarborough, 1998).

Background knowledge is also very important to constructing the meaning of text, but difficult to measure. Individuals who are proficient at comprehending a written text make connections within and across texts. This integration of information requires background knowledge from a variety of sources on a range of topics. In addition, children need to have a schema for the various situations elaborated in a text. For example, a story about a library or a zoo requires some level of knowledge about those places. Children with more elaborate schemas will have a deeper level of comprehension than children with little to no background knowledge about those places. It is also important for children to realize when their schemas are incorrect or incomplete and to assimilate the new information.

In sum, a broad array of skills influences early reading development. Numerous groups have argued that multivariate approaches to screening increases accuracy beyond reliance on any single test or measure (Compton, Fuchs, Fuchs, & Bryant, 2006; Fletcher et al., 2002; Francis, Fletcher, Catts, & Tomblin, 2005; McCardle et al., 2001). Therefore, we recommend using screening batteries during the RTI process that include multiple tasks, rather than single-task instruments. Screening batteries should include a mixture of seven broad skills areas that relate to future reading skill: (a) phonological skills, (b) orthographic knowledge, (c) letter knowledge, (d) word reading ability, (e) vocabulary, (f) syntactic ability, and (g) background knowledge. Each of these skills is influenced by development; consequently, the items on the screener should vary as a function of age and reading development. A screener's effectiveness depends not only on how well it evaluates behaviors, but also on how well a measure is incorporated into the response to intervention process.

IMPROVING THE ACCURACY OF SCREENING DECISIONS

The accuracy of RD risk determination can be improved by diversifying the screening information to include family risk factors, focusing on first-grade children, and conducting short-term progress monitoring to gauge student response to the general education curriculum.

Diversifying Screening Information

Influential variables such as home environment and attention/behavior ratings tend to be left off of classroom-based screeners in favor of language-based tasks, with the assumption that these measures do not provide enough predictive value to warrant the extra time and resources required for their administration. To the contrary, studies have reported that phonological skills and home background factors are reliable predictors of early reading development (Vellutino et al., 1996).

Home background variables such as socioeconomic status (SES) and home literacy environment have predictive validity in identifying students who may fail to respond properly to intervention (Foorman et al., 1997). Snow, Barnes, Chandler, Goodman, and Hemphill (1991) noted that parent education and income was highly associated with student achievement, more so than school or classroom factors. Parent income and education and student eligibility for free or reduced lunch are used most frequently in research to approximate student SES. Whether students qualify for free or reduced lunch tends to have a slightly higher relation to academic achievement than parent income, education, or occupation (Sirin, 2005). Sirin noted that although SES measures have proven to be reliable predictors across studies, measures of home background variables such as number of books in home, availability of computers, and other educational resources have also proven to be good predictors. The relation between these home background variables and achievement is strongest when the data are collected directly from parents, as opposed to secondary sources or students (Sirin); a parental survey is the most efficient means of gathering this information.

Many genetic factors also influence reading ability, and some of these factors interact with one another and with the environment. An estimated 30% to 70% of the variability in performance on measures of reading ability is genetically determined (Pennington & Olson, 2005). Pennington and Lefly (2001) reported that children without a reading disability diagnosis who had a parent or sibling with a diagnosed reading disability scored significantly lower than same age controls on measures of basic literacy skills such as reading and spelling. Therefore, family history of a reading problem can be a powerful tool to predict at-risk status, especially when used in conjunction with assessments of linguistic and cognitive skills.

A child's attention and behavior in the classroom environment are also highly predictive of future language and literacy growth. Teacher ratings of student attention and behavior are highly effective predictors of future reading ability and growth (Stage, Abbott, Jenkins, & Berninger, 2003). Attention is important because of its relevance to attention deficit/hyperactivity disorder (ADHD), but even in children without an ADHD diagnosis, attention explains significant variance in word reading task after accounting for age. Given the high percentages of reported false negatives and false positives when using just language and print knowledge to predict risk, teacher ratings of student behavior and attention should also be included in the assessment battery.

Focusing on First-Grade Children

Research shows that accurate determination of the risk pool tends to increase as children experience more reading instruction, leading some to suggest that screening should occur at the beginning of first grade rather than in kindergarten (Fletcher et al., 2002). Increased power to classify correctly first-grade children as at risk for RD likely comes from three sources (Fletcher et al.):

- The collection of first-grade screening measures expands to include skills more closely aligned with reading (e.g., word identification and nonword decoding).

- Initial differences among kindergarten children due to variation in family literacy practices may diminish with formal kindergarten instruction.

- Measurement precision increases with age as intrachild instability decreases.

Despite the benefits of waiting another year, the accuracy of determining risk among first graders is still less than ideal. Simply waiting to screen until the beginning of first grade will likely be insufficient to improve the accuracy of RD risk determination to a level that is required within an RTI model. We recognize the tension created by waiting to make risk designations in first grade versus making decisions in kindergarten, allowing early preventive intervention. It therefore may make sense to identify and give support to those children most at risk for developing reading difficulties in kindergarten, and monitor the progress of the remaining risk pool into first grade.

Children's Response to General Education Curriculum

A third approach for increasing the accuracy of RD risk designation is short-term progress monitoring (i.e., 5–10 weeks into first grade). Inadequate response to classroom instruction, as revealed by slope and/or level, should indicate risk for poor long-term outcome beyond that associated with initial screening performance (e.g., L. S. Fuchs & Fuchs, 1998). L. S. Fuchs, Fuchs, and Compton (2004) reported that growth (i.e., slope) on a measure of word identification fluency correlated strongly with end-of-first-grade word identification, passage reading fluency, and passage comprehension. In addition, Compton et al. (2006) demonstrated that using progress monitoring data from the beginning of first grade significantly improved the ability to predict who would develop RD at the end of second grade. Even so, very few studies have examined the utility of using short-term progress monitoring as a strategy for determining long-term outcome, or how progress monitoring might be used in combination with other screening measures to improve decision accuracy; this is an important avenue for future research.

FINAL THOUGHTS

Although an RTI approach has undeniable advantages over traditional IQ–achievement discrepancy procedures, its effectiveness is dependent on the accurate and efficient identification of a risk pool of children who enter Tier 2 intervention. Given that reading development is influenced by a broad array of developmentally influenced skills, screening batteries must vary according to children's reading development. Schools can improve the accuracy of identifying children in need of Tier 2 intervention by instituting early screening that focuses on the areas of phonological skills, orthographic knowledge, letter knowledge, word reading ability, vocabulary, syntactic ability, and background knowledge. Moreover, schools should take into account that academic performance is influenced significantly by home environment, and factor variables such as number of books in the home and the occurrence of reading disability in other family members into the risk calculation. Finally, progress monitoring techniques will help to accurately gauge children's response to the general education curriculum.

REFERENCES

Adams, M. J. (1990). *Beginning to read: Thinking and learning about print*. Cambridge, MA: MIT Press.

Bradley, R., Danielson, L., & Hallahan, D. P. (Eds.). (2002). *Identification of learning disabilities: Research to practice*. Mahwah, NJ: Lawrence Erlbaum.

Compton, D. L. (2000). Modeling the growth of decoding skills in first-grade children. *Scientific Studies of Reading 4*(3), 219–258.

Compton, D. L., & Carlisle, J. F. (1994). Speed of word recognition as a distinguishing characteristic of reading disabilities. *Educational Psychology Review, 6*(2), 115–140.

Compton, D. L., Fuchs, D., Fuchs, L. S., & Bryant, J. D. (2006). Selecting at-risk readers in first grade for early intervention: A two-year longitudinal study of decision rules and procedures. *Journal of Educational Psychology, 98*(2), 394–409.

Elbro, C., & Scarborough, H. (2004). Early identification. In P. Bryant & T. Nunes (Eds.), *International handbook of children's literacy* (pp. 319–359). Dordrecht, The Netherlands: Kluwer.

Fletcher, J. M., Foorman, B. R., Boudousquie, A., Barnes, M., Schatschneider, C., & Francis, D. (2002). Assessment of reading and learning disabilities: A research-based intervention-oriented approach. *Journal of School Psychology, 40*(1), 27–63.

Foorman, B. R., Francis, D. J., Winikates, D., Mehta, P., Schatschneider, C., & Fletcher, J. M. (1997). Early interventions for children with reading disabilities. *Scientific Studies of Reading, 1*(3), 255–276.

Francis, D. J., Fletcher, J. M., Catts, H., & Tomblin, B. (2005). Dimensions affecting the assessment of reading comprehension. In S. G. Paris & S. A. Stahl (Eds.), *Children's reading comprehension and assessment* (pp. 369–394). Mahwah, NJ: Lawrence Erlbaum.

Fuchs, D., Mock, D., Morgan, P. L., & Young, C. (2003). Responsiveness-to-intervention: Definitions, evidence, and implications for the learning disabilities construct. *Learning Disabilities Research and Practice, 18*(3), 157–171.

Fuchs, L. S., & Fuchs, D. (1998). Treatment validity: A unifying concept for reconceptualizing identification of learning disabilities. *Learning Disabilities Research & Practice, 13*(4), 204–219.

Fuchs, L. S., Fuchs, D., & Compton, D. L. (2004). Monitoring early reading development in first grade: Word identification fluency versus nonsense word fluency. *Exceptional Children, 71*, 7–21.

Gough, P. B., & Tunmer, W. E. (1986). Decoding, reading and reading disability. *Remedial and Special Education, 7*(1), 6–10.

Jenkins, J. R., & O'Connor, R. E. (2002). Early identification and intervention for young children with reading/learning disabilities. In R. Bradley, L. Danielson, & D. Hallahan (Eds.), *Identification of learning disabilities: Research to practice* (pp. 99–149). Mahwah, NJ: Lawrence Erlbaum.

McCardle, P., Scarborough, H., & Catts, H. (2001). Predicting, explaining, and preventing children's reading difficulties. *Learning Disabilities Research & Practice, 16*(4), 230–239.

Pennington, B. F., & Lefly, D. L. (2001). Early reading development in children at family risk for dyslexia. *Child Development, 72*(3), 816–833.

Pennington, B. F., & Olson, R. K. (2005). Genetics of dyslexia. In M. J. Snowling & C. Hulme (Eds.), *The science of reading: A handbook* (pp. 453–472). Oxford, England: Blackwell.

Scarborough, H. S. (1991). Antecedents to reading disability: Preschool language development and literacy experiences of children from dyslexic families. *Reading and Writing: An Interdisciplinary Journal, 3,* 219–223.

Scarborough, H. S. (1998). Predicting the future achievement of second graders with reading disabilities: Contributions of phonemic awareness, verbal memory, rapid naming, and IQ. *Annals of Dyslexia, 68,* 115–136.

Schatschneider, C., Francis, D. J., Foorman, B. R., Fletcher, J. M., & Mehta, P. (1999). The dimensionality of phonological awareness: An application of item response theory. *Journal of Educational Psychology, 91,* 439–449.

Share, D. L., Jorm, A. F., Maclean, R., & Matthews, R. (1984). Sources of individual differences in reading acquisition. *Journal of Educational Psychology, 76,* 1309–1324.

Share, D. L., Jorm, A. F., Maclean, R., & Matthews, R. (2002). Temporal processing and reading disability. *Reading and Writing: An Interdisciplinary Journal, 15,* 151–178.

Sirin, S. R. (2005). Socioeconomic status and academic achievement: A meta-analytic review of research. *Review of Educational Research, 75*(3), 417–453.

Snow, C., Barnes, W. S., Chandler, J., Goodman, I. F., & Hemphill, L. (1991). *Unfulfilled expectations: Home and school influences on literacy.* Cambridge, MA: Harvard University Press.

Stage, S. A., Abbott, R. D., Jenkins, J. R., & Berninger, V. W. (2003). Predicting response to early reading intervention from verbal IQ, reading-related language abilities, attention ratings, and verbal IQ-word reading discrepancy: Failure to validate discrepancy method. *Journal of Learning Disabilities, 36*(1), 24–33.

Torgesen, J. K. (2002). The prevention of reading difficulties. *Journal of School Psychology, 40*(1), 7–26.

Treiman, R. (1993). *Beginning to spell: A study of first-grade children.* New York: Oxford University Press.

Treiman, R., Weatherston, S., & Berch, D. (1994). The role of letter names in children's learning of phoneme-grapheme relations. *Applied Psycholinguistics, 15,* 97–122.

Vaughn, S., & Fuchs, L. S. (2003). Redefining learning disabilities as inadequate response to instruction: The promise and potential problems. *Learning Disabilities Research & Practice, 18*(3), 137–146.

Vellutino F. R., Scanlon, D. M., Sipay, E. R., Small, S. G., Pratt, A., Chen, R., & Denckla, M. B. (1996). Cognitive profiles of difficult-to-remediate and readily remediated poor readers: Early intervention as a vehicle for distinguishing between cognitive and experiential deficits as basic causes of specific reading disability. *Journal of Educational Psychology, 88,* 601–638.

This research was supported in part by Grant #H324U010004 from the U.S. Department of Education, Office of Special Education Programs, and NIH Grants P30HD15052 and the Roadmap for Medical Research T32MH75883 to Vanderbilt University. Statements do not reflect the position or policy of these agencies, and no official endorsement by them should be inferred.

Originally published in *TEACHING Exceptional Children,* Vol. 39, No. 5, pp. 32–37.

6

Secondary Interventions in Reading: Providing Additional Instruction for Students At Risk

Sharon Vaughn and Greg Roberts

Leon McBride is an elementary school principal who was previously a special education teacher. He comments about Responsiveness to Intervention (RTI), "I have heard a great deal about RTI as part of the newly reauthorized law for special education students. However, I am responsible for all of the learners in my school. How does RTI fit into the entire school context? What can I do, as the curriculum leader for my school, to implement the most effective interventions so that I know what responsiveness *means in my school?"*

This article is designed to help Leon McBride, as well as other educational leaders and teachers, better understand how they might build an integrated approach—general and special education working together—to implementing RTI. Fundamentally, a three-tiered system provides a framework that allows for all students to be provided with universal screening and appropriate classroom-based instruction as part of primary prevention (Tier 1). Secondary intervention (Tier 2) is provided for those students for whom primary prevention (Tier 1) is not sufficient and who require additional instruction in the target area (e.g., reading; Reschly, 2005). Tertiary intervention (Tier 3) provides even more intensive intervention and more frequent progress monitoring and is designed for those students for whom secondary intervention was inadequate.

According to Reschly (2005), the primary differences between the tiers are "intervention intensity and measurement precision" (p. 511). This article will focus on secondary prevention within a three-tiered system, where as many as 20% to 30% of students (depending upon the effectiveness of the Tier 1 instruction) will require supplemental intervention.

WHAT IS SECONDARY PREVENTION/TIER 2?

Secondary preventions are intervention practices directed at students who are at risk for academic problems and for whom additional, more targeted instruction is provided to close the gap between their current performance and expected performance. Figure 1 highlights some important differences between secondary prevention and tertiary prevention: (a) students typically served in secondary interventions may have less severe problems than students in tertiary interventions; (b) more intensive interventions are provided in tertiary programs—intensity can be defined as duration of the intervention as well as group size; and (c) the expertise of individuals providing the intervention may vary, with teachers providing tertiary interventions demonstrating very high levels of expertise and knowledge.

Figure 1 summarizes one way of conceptualizing secondary interventions within a three-tiered model. This figure provides guidelines for how a school or district might address many of the critical questions that relate to the delivery of secondary interventions, including: (a) who provides the intervention, (b) what elements of instruction the intervention addresses, (c) how much time will the intervention be delivered, and (d) how we know when a student demonstrates adequate response to the intervention. Figure 1 also addresses issues related to each tier of instruction and provides a comparison across tiers of intervention.

WHO PROVIDES THE SECONDARY INTERVENTION?

For secondary interventions, students benefit when personnel are highly trained to implement the specified intervention. With this in mind, a range of possible personnel might provide secondary interventions. Decisions about who implements the intervention are related to district/school practices and resources: Some schools or districts will use certified teachers and some will use paraprofessionals supervised by teachers. Any of the following personnel might effectively implement secondary prevention interventions: (a) certified teachers, (b) reading specialists, (c) trained tutors/paraprofessionals, or (d) classroom teachers who coordinate implementation of secondary interventions with their same-grade teachers.

Although most districts/schools might prefer highly trained and certified teachers to provide secondary interventions, research indicates that well-trained tutors/paraprofessionals are associated with improved outcomes for students as long as they are provided extensive and ongoing professional development, support and coaching, and clear guidance on instructional

Figure 1. Overview of Tiers 1, 2, and 3

	Tier 1	Tier 2	Tier 3
Definition	Reading instruction and programs, including ongoing professional development and benchmark assessments (3 times per year)	Instructional intervention employed to supplement, enhance, and support Tier 1; takes place in small groups	Individualized reading instruction extended beyond the time allocated for Tier 1; groups of 1–3 students
Focus	All students	Students identified with reading difficulties who have not responded to Tier 1 efforts	Students with marked difficulties in reading or reading disabilities who have not responded adequately to Tier 1 and Tier 2 efforts
Program	Scientifically based reading instruction and curriculum emphasizing the critical elements.	Specialized, scientifically based reading instruction and curriculum emphasizing the critical elements	Sustained, intensive, scientifically based reading instruction and curriculum highly responsive to students' needs
Instruction	Sufficient opportunities to practice throughout the school day	• Additional attention, focus, support • Additional opportunities to practice embedded throughout the day • Preteach, review skills; frequent opportunities to practice skills	Carefully designed and implemented, explicit, systematic instruction
Interventionist	General education teacher	Personnel determined by the school (classroom teacher, specialized reading teacher, other trained personnel)	Personnel determined by the school (e.g., specialized reading teacher, special education teacher)
Setting	General education classroom	Appropriate setting designated by the school	Appropriate setting designated by the school
Grouping	Flexible grouping	Homogeneous small-group instruction (e.g., 1:4, 1:5)	Homogeneous small-group instruction (1:2, 1:3)
Time	Minimum of 90 min per day	20–30 min per day in addition to Tier 1	50-min sessions (or longer) per day depending upon appropriateness of Tier 1
Assessment	Benchmark assessments at beginning, middle, and end of academic year	Progress monitoring twice a month on target skill to ensure adequate progress and learning	Progress monitoring at least twice a month on target skill to ensure adequate progress and learning

Note: Adapted from Vaughn Gross Center for Reading and Language Arts at The University of Texas at Austin. (2005). *Implementing the 3-tier reading model: Reducing reading difficulties for kindergarten through third grade students* (2nd ed.). Austin, TX: Author.

practices (Elbaum, Vaughn, Hughes, & Moody, 2000; Vaughn & Linan-Thompson, 2003). Furthermore, according to the Individuals With Disabilities Education Improvement Act of 2004 (IDEA), up to 15% of special education funds can be used to implement prevention practices such as those provided through secondary intervention.

WHAT ELEMENTS OF INSTRUCTION DO INTERVENTIONS ADDRESS?

Research suggests that there are identifiable elements of reading instruction associated with improved outcomes for students at risk for reading problems (National Institute of Child Health and Human Development, 2000; Snow, Burns, & Griffin, 1998; Swanson & Hoskyn, 1998; Vaughn, Gersten, & Chard, 2000), including phonemic awareness, phonics, spelling and writing, fluency, vocabulary, and comprehension.

When selecting or developing secondary interventions, it is critical to remember that the goal is that students will "catch up" with their peers after secondary intervention, which is typically implemented in 20- to 30-min sessions over a period of 10 to 20 weeks. For secondary interventions to be effective, instructional time during interventions needs to be highly focused and keenly aligned with the instructional needs of the student. The extent to which each of these elements is emphasized is related to the student's instructional level. The key elements of early reading included in secondary interventions are (see Figure 2, "Guidelines for Secondary Interventions in Reading Instruction"):

- *Phonemic awareness instruction,* teaching students to understand the sounds of language and to manipulate them in ways that are associated with improved reading.

- *Phonics instruction,* teaching students how to link the sounds of language to print, to recognize words based on recognized patterns, to decode multisyllabic words, and to generalize the learned rules of language to new words.

- *Spelling/writing instruction,* used to support the acquisition of phonics rules and word reading. Many students benefit when they have ample practice hearing sounds and then writing them. Mapping sounds to print and teaching students to recognize word patterns (e.g., *am, it, ate, eed*) helps students read words rapidly. Thus, encouraging students to write letters, sound patterns, words, and sentences during secondary intervention yields improved outcomes for reading.

- *Fluency instruction,* teaching students to read words accurately and with sufficient speed that comprehension is not impaired because of undue focus on word reading.

Figure 2. Guidelines for Secondary Interventions in Reading Instruction

Phonemic Awareness	**Teach phonemic awareness early** to students who need it. Students can be exposed to beginning phonemic awareness activities as early as preschool and are likely to benefit from phonemic awareness through initial reading. **Ensure that phonemic awareness instruction is fun** and involves interesting and engaging activities. • Phonemic awareness activities can be made easier by using larger chunks (like syllables) and then more difficult by asking students to blend and segment phonemes. • Teach phonemic awareness with letter sounds and showing students letters. **Assess students frequently** to assure progress. Encourage the connection between sounds and markers (initially) and then later sounds and letters. (Jenkins & O'Connor, 2002)
Phonics	**From the very beginning,** • Teach students to link phonemes (sounds) to graphemes (letters) explicitly from the very beginning (Jenkins & O'Connor, 2002). • Ask students to write letters that represent sounds. • Encourage students to write and spell words. **Teach students to say the words** quickly if they can but when needed, encourage them to "sound out" the words. **Provide students with many opportunities** to read words and sentences that correspond with the phonics elements they are learning. **Teach students explicitly how to chunk and read** multisyllable words. **Help students understand affixes and root words** so that they can both read the words and know what they mean.
Spelling and Writing	**Provide students with ample opportunity** to see and write the letters, letter combinations, and words that are associated with the sounds they are learning from the beginning of secondary intervention. **Give students opportunities to practice** writing and reading words with common word patterns (e.g., sat, man, mit, bed, up, lot) as well as irregular words (e.g., was, from, the). **Provide students with tasks** that allow them to write as many words as they can that conform to the rule patterns learned. **Allow students to write sentences** and responses related to what they read.
Fluency	**Support fluency through repeated reading,** including choral reading, paired reading, audiotapes, and computer reading. **Allow students to take turns reading** so that they are given a break after every paragraph or two; many students who require secondary interventions are often challenged by reading large amounts of text. **Assess students' text reading regularly** to ensure that their speed is sufficient for understanding text. **Prepare students** for text reading by reviewing high-frequency words.
Vocabulary	**Identify and preteach** key vocabulary words related to what students are reading. **Review word meaning** throughout instruction. **Encourage students to be word detectives** who are interested in new words, their meanings, and how they relate to existing words.

continues

Figure 2. *Continued*

Comprehension	**Before reading,** activate the students' background knowledge for the selected passage, assisting students in thinking about how this text may be related to other texts in terms of content, storyline, and text structure. Prereading activities (Graves, Juel, & Graves, 2001): • motivate and set purposes for reading • activate and build background knowledge • build text-specific knowledge • relate reading to students' lives • provide opportunities for prequestioning, predicting, and direction setting. **During reading,** encourage students to self-question and monitor their comprehension as they read, and model/think-aloud comprehension strategies that you want students to use, including • asking simple and increasingly more complex questions, including those that have the answers in the text and those that require students to link previous information with what they are reading • asking relevant questions that promote understanding, such as who, what, when, where, why, and how questions • checking for understanding and using "fix-up" strategies while reading to facilitate comprehension. **After reading,** give students opportunities to respond orally and in writing to what they've read, including • teaching for generalization (i.e., when and where strategies apply) and maintenance • clarifying unclear concepts or vocabulary • summarizing by determining the main ideas and important concepts related to the main idea • discussing the content of the reading as well as evaluating the writing style • assisting students in summarizing and organizing what they have read. (Mastropieri & Scruggs, 1997; Pressley, 2006; Swanson, 1999; Vaughn & Linan-Thompson, 2004)

- *Vocabulary instruction,* teaching students to recognize the meaning of words they are reading and to build an appreciation of new words and their meaning so that learning the meaning of new words is an ongoing process supported by the teacher and through independent activities.

- *Comprehension instruction,* teaching students to monitor their understanding while reading, linking what they read to previous learning, asking questions about what they read, and responding to what they read in increasingly more sophisticated ways.

Remember, not all elements may be appropriate for all students and all levels of development. Students who are already reading words will not require phonemic awareness and students who do not know letters, sounds, and word reading would not require reading comprehension.

HOW INTENSIVE SHOULD SECONDARY INTERVENTIONS BE?

Two of the ways to make interventions more intense are to decrease the group size so that fewer students are with each teacher and to increase the "dosage," or amount of intervention provided. When we think about intensity, we need to consider grouping practices and amount of intervention. With respect to grouping practices, few teachers would deny that one-on-one instruction is the preferred instructional group size. However, few schools have resources to afford this level of intensity, particularly for secondary interventions; it is much more likely that schools will provide secondary interventions in group sizes of 3 to 6 students.

When we consider the "intensity" of the intervention, we also think about (a) amount of time per day, (b) number of days per week, (c) the number of weeks of instruction, and (d) when instruction will occur—before, during, or after school. One model for providing secondary intervention is to instruct students in groups of 3 to 5 for each teacher, every day, for approximately 30 min. This same model could be adjusted so that the secondary intervention occurred before or after school. It is also feasible to implement the secondary intervention for longer time (for example, 45 min per day) for fewer days (3–4 days per week). The intervention must be intensive enough to provide students with a reasonable opportunity to "catch up" to grade-level expectations. Students should not be "locked into" the secondary intervention for long periods of time without ongoing progress monitoring and consideration of their trajectory for meeting grade-level expectations.

EFFECTIVE SECONDARY INTERVENTIONS FOR STUDENTS AT RISK FOR READING PROBLEMS

There are numerous examples of programs/curricula associated with improved outcomes for students who are monolingual English readers (e.g., Foorman, 2003; Kamps & Greenwood, 2005; Torgesen, 2000), as well as for students who are English language learners (e.g., Vaughn, Linan-Thompson et al., 2006; Vaughn, Mathes et al., 2006). The elements of effective instruction described previously in this article provide guidelines for selecting programs and designing curricula. In addition to the key elements of instruction, students benefit from interventions that

- Use appropriate grouping formats.
- Provide targeted instruction three to five times per week.
- Assure additional instruction aligns with core reading instruction.
- Provide ongoing and systematic corrective feedback to students.
- Provide extended practice in the critical components of reading instruction based on students' needs.
- Increase time for word study, fluency, and comprehension.

- Use systematic classroom-based instructional assessment to document student growth and inform instruction.

DETERMINING ADEQUATE RESPONSE TO SECONDARY INTERVENTIONS

Students receiving secondary intervention in reading are likely to fall into one of three broad categories (Vaughn, Linan-Thompson, & Hickman, 2003). Some students provided secondary intervention will make significant progress after they are provided 50 to 100 sessions of intervention so that they are no longer in the "risk" category for reading problems. Some students will make progress, but it will not be enough to "catch up" with their classmates or with expected levels of performance. A minority, less than 10% of all secondary intervention students, may make little or no substantial progress when provided with a research-based, standardized intervention.

Having timely and reliable information on how students respond during secondary intervention is essential to making sound and timely decisions about future instruction (Fuchs & Fuchs, 2002). Students whose response to intervention is substantial and sufficient, for example, may be candidates for "graduation" from secondary intervention, though it would be prudent to continue monitoring their response to core instruction to ensure that they do not require secondary intervention at a later time. Some students in the second group—students who exhibit some progress but have not "caught up"— may benefit from continuing in the secondary intervention if there is evidence that they are making good progress. An alternative instructional program or referral to special education may be appropriate for students in this group not making adequate progress and for students who made little or no substantial progress.

Progress monitoring linked to explicit and direct instruction is a primary means of making reliable instructional and placement decisions (Stecker & Fuchs, 2000). Progress monitoring measures are easily and quickly administered. They provide a "snapshot" of student response at points throughout an instructional sequence. Progress monitoring offers a means of tracking progress over time (Deno, Fuchs, Marston, & Shin, 2001) and of evaluating the relationship of a given rate of progress compared with the rate necessary to meet grade-level expectations. Progress monitoring measures can be given repeatedly, within a narrow time period, without compromising their usefulness, unlike most end-of-chapter and teacher-made tests. Progress monitoring data yield information within a matter of hours, distinguishing them from most end-of-year standardized tests, the scores of which are typically not available until the following school year. Well-designed progress monitoring measures provide reliable and relevant information for making instructional decisions and for refining instructional plans (Marston, Mirkin, & Deno, 1984).

Fuchs (2003) identifies three primary considerations when planning and implementing a system of progress monitoring:

Key Elements of Secondary Interventions in Reading

> ✓ Conduct an initial assessment to identify students who need intervention and to determine students' needs.
>
> ✓ Form same-ability small groups.
>
> ✓ Provide daily, targeted instruction that is explicit, systematic, and provides ample practice opportunities with immediate feedback.
>
> ✓ Focus on the most important instructional elements based on the students' grade level and expertise.
>
> ✓ Determine the readability of texts to ensure that students are reading texts at the appropriate level of difficulty.
>
> ✓ Match reading levels to the purpose for reading.
>
> ✓ Provide many opportunities for struggling readers to apply what they are learning as they read words, word lists, and sentences in texts.
>
> ✓ Include a writing component based on students' abilities.
>
> ✓ Involve parents and other caregivers so that they can support their students' efforts by listening to them read and discuss with them what they are reading.
>
> ✓ Conduct frequent progress monitoring (e.g., every 2 weeks) to track student progress and inform instruction and grouping.
>
> *Note.* From Vaughn Gross Center for Reading and Language Arts, 2005.

(1) Alignment between what is taught and what is measured: As a rule, the two should be significantly aligned. In the case of early reading, measures of word identification, phonemic decoding, text-reading fluency, vocabulary, and reading comprehension would be appropriate.

(2) Timing and frequency of measurement: More at-risk students, those in groups two and three, should be monitored more frequently, perhaps as often as weekly.

(3) Determining "adequate response" through use of a well-developed and validated system of measures.

ISSUES TO CONSIDER

Gerber (2005) states that there are two important determinants of student success: opportunity to learn and quality of instruction. RTI must have a feasible method of addressing these two elements if its application is to be successful. Essential to the successful implementation of RTI is a systemic and standardized approach to providing secondary interventions for students at risk. The "scale up" of these standardized secondary interventions in natural settings may not be easy to implement, and many schools will be challenged to establish the necessary procedures and practices for implementation of effective secondary interventions (Denton, Vaughn, & Fletcher, 2003).

The number of students requiring secondary interventions is related to the quality of the core instruction provided (Kamps & Greenwood, 2005); high-risk schools that use inappropriate instruction are likely to have many students who require secondary intervention. An essential component of successful RTI implementation is leadership that is knowledgeable and supportive of the development and implementation of secondary interventions. Thus, there are several key considerations for effectively implementing secondary interventions: (a) leadership that is committed to prevention-oriented practices, (b) curriculum leaders who are willing to assure that scientifically based research practices are implemented, (c) ongoing professional development to assure knowledgeable personnel are implementing secondary interventions, and (d) use of ongoing assessments to determine student progress and adjust instructional decisions.

REFERENCES

Deno, S. L., Fuchs, L. S., Marston, D., & Shin, J. (2001). Using curriculum-based measurement to establish growth standards for students with learning disabilities. *School Psychology Review, 30*(4), 507–524.

Denton, C. A., Vaughn, S., & Fletcher, J. M. (2003). Bringing research-based practices in reading intervention to scale. *Learning Disabilities Research & Practice, 18*, 201–211.

Elbaum, B., Vaughn, S., Hughes, M. T., & Moody, S. W. (2000). How effective are one-to-one tutoring programs in reading for elementary students at risk for reading failure? *Journal of Educational Psychology, 92*(4), 605–619.

Foorman, B. (Ed.). (2003). *Preventing and remediating reading difficulties: Bringing science to scale.* Baltimore, MD: York Press.

Fuchs, L. (2003). Assessing intervention responsiveness: Conceptual and technical issues. *Learning Disabilities Research and Practice. 18*(3), 172–186.

Fuchs, L. S., & Fuchs, D. (2002). Curriculum-based measurement: Describing competence, enhancing outcomes, evaluating treatment effects, and identifying treatment nonresponders. *Peabody Journal of Education, 77*, 64–84.

Gerber, M. (2005). Teachers are still the test: Limitations of Response to Instruction strategies for identifying children with learning disabilities. *Journal of Learning Disabilities, 38*(6), 516–524.

Graves, M., Juel, C., & Graves, B. (2001). *Teaching reading in the 21st century.* Des Moines, IA: Allyn & Bacon.

Jenkins, J. R., & O'Connor, R. E. (2002). Early identification and intervention for young children with reading/learning disabilities. In R. Bradley, L. Danielson, & D. P. Hallahan (Eds.), *Identification of learning disabilities: Research to practice* (pp. 99–149). Mahwah, NJ: Erlbaum.

Kamps, D. M., & Greenwood, C. R. (2005). Formulating secondary-level reading interventions. *Journal of Learning Disabilities, 38*(6), 500–509.

Marston, D., Mirkin, P. K., & Deno, S. L. (1984). Curriculum-based measurement: An alternative to traditional screening, referral, and identification. *Journal of Special Education, 19*, 109–118.

Mastropieri, M. A., & Scruggs, T. E. (1997). Best practices in promoting reading comprehension in students with learning disabilities: 1976 to 1996. *Remedial and Special Education, 18*(4), 197–214.

National Institute of Child Health and Human Development. (2000). *Report of the National Reading Panel. Teaching children to read: An evidence-based assessment of the scientific research literature on reading and its implications for reading instruction* (NIH Publication No. 00-4769). Washington, DC: U.S. Government Printing Office.

Pressley, M. (2006). *Reading instruction that works: The case for balanced teaching.* New York: Guilford.

Reschly, D. (2005). Learning disabilities: Primary intervention, secondary intervention, and then what? *Journal of Learning Disabilities, 38*(6), 510–515.

Snow, C., Burns, S., & Griffin, P. (1998). *Preventing reading difficulties in young children.* Washington, DC: National Research Council.

Stecker, P. M., & Fuchs, L. S. (2000). Effecting superior achievement using curriculum-based measurement: The importance of individual progress monitoring. *Learning Disabilities Research and Practice, 15*, 128–134.

Swanson, H. L. (1999). Instructional components that predict treatment outcomes for students with learning disabilities: Support for a combined strategy and direct instruction model. *Learning Disabilities Research & Practice, 14*(3), 129–140.

Swanson, H. L., & Hoskyn, M. (1998). Experimental intervention research on students with learning disabilities: A meta-analysis of treatment outcomes. *Review of Educational Research, 68*(3), 277–321.

Torgesen, J. K. (2000). Individual differences in response to early interventions in reading: The lingering problem of treatment resisters. *Learning Disabilities Research & Practice, 15*, 55–64.

Vaughn Gross Center for Reading and Language Arts at The University of Texas at Austin. (2005). *Implementing the 3-tier reading model: Reducing reading difficulties for kindergarten through third grade students* (2nd ed.). Austin, TX: Author.

Vaughn, S., Gersten, R., & Chard, D. J. (2000). The underlying message in LD intervention research: Findings from research syntheses. *Exceptional Children, 67*(1), 99–114.

Vaughn, S., & Linan-Thompson, S. (2003). Group size and time allotted to intervention: Effects for students with reading difficulties. In B. Foorman (Ed.), *Preventing and remediating reading difficulties: Bringing science to scale* (pp. 275–298). Parkton, MD: York Press.

Vaughn, S., & Linan-Thompson, S. (2004). *Research-based methods of reading instruction: Grades K–3.* Alexandria, VA: Association for Supervision and Curriculum Development.

Vaughn, S., Linan-Thompson, S., & Hickman, P. (2003). Response to instruction as a means of identifying students with reading/learning disabilities. *Exceptional Children, 69*, 391–409.

Vaughn, S., Linan-Thompson, S., Mathes, P. G., Cirino, P. T., Carlson, C. D., Pollard-Durodola, S. D., et al. (2006). Effectiveness of Spanish intervention for first-grade English language learners at risk for reading difficulties. *Journal of Learning Disabilities, 39*(1), 56–73.

Vaughn, S., Mathes, P. G., Linan-Thompson, S., Cirino, P. T., Carlson, C. D., Pollard-Durodola, S. D., et al. (2006). First-grade English language learners at-risk for reading problems: Effectiveness of an English intervention. *Elementary School Journal, 107*(2), 153–180.

Originally published in *TEACHING Exceptional Children,* Vol. 39, No. 5, pp. 40–46.

Tertiary Intervention: Using Progress Monitoring With Intensive Services

Pamela M. Stecker

In a Responsiveness-to-Intervention (RTI) model, successive levels of instructional supports based on scientifically sound practices are provided to students who experience academic difficulties. Although professionals have described specific components of the RTI multi-tiered system in different ways, authors of the RTI series in this issue describe a three-tiered system of instructional service to students who struggle academically, including the identification and provision of special education to students with specific learning disabilities (SLD). What is common across discussions of RTI as a prevention–intervention model is that increasingly more intensive instructional support is provided during each successive tier to students who are designated as at risk or when these students demonstrate academic unresponsiveness in previous tiers. The third tier, or tertiary intervention, is the main focus of this article. In this model, Tier 3 includes the provision of special education services.

Under the Individuals With Disabilities Education Improvement Act of 2004, states may no longer require the use of the discrepancy approach (i.e., between intellectual functioning and achievement) to identify individuals with SLD. The law permits states and districts to use data from student response to research-based interventions, such as those collected through an RTI approach, as an alternative route for identifying SLD. Although RTI practices have been in place in some locations for a number of years (see e.g., D. Fuchs, Mock, Morgan, & Young, 2003; Marston, Muyskens, Lau, & Canter, 2003; Tilly,

2006; Vaughn & Chard, 2006), no standard protocol has been mandated for directing the RTI process. Consequently, current models vary with respect to particular features of the model. What is common among approaches, however, is that progress-monitoring data are used for decision-making purposes. Data aid teachers in making judgments about the success of their instruction for individual students and to determine when additional support is needed, or conversely, when such intensive instruction no longer is needed because a student has responded well to intervention. For example, when progress-monitoring data illustrate good response to secondary prevention services (i.e., Tier 2), the student may be moved back to primary prevention (i.e., Tier 1). Progress monitoring continues, and, if the student experiences a serious lag in academic achievement, Tier 2 intervening support may be necessary again. In this way, progress-monitoring data support flexibility within the RTI model for moving a student back and forth through tiers and become central to RTI practices.

The following section briefly reviews typical practices in Tiers 1 and 2 and describes how tertiary instruction (i.e., Tier 3) differs from previous tiers. In this model, intensive tertiary intervention includes the provision of special education. Next, the RTI process is described in the context of a classroom scenario with a hypothetical student who struggles significantly with reading. This case study illustrates how progress-monitoring data are used to move this student through the RTI tiers and subsequently to aid in identifying her as having an SLD. Within tertiary intervention, progress-monitoring data are used in a variety of ways: to develop an individualized education program (IEP) goal, to judge the adequacy of student progress and the success of the instructional program, to determine when instructional changes appear necessary, and to formulate instructional modifications to better meet individual needs. Moreover, when data indicate substantial improvement in level and rate of progress, students may be moved out of tertiary intervention into a less intensive instructional tier. Finally, several remaining questions regarding RTI practices and challenges for implementation are discussed.

OVERVIEW OF TIERS

General Description of Tier 1

Universal screening may be a part of Tier 1 or is completed routinely prior to the implementation of Tier 1 interventions. Benchmark scores, results on standardized achievement tests, or median scores from several progress-monitoring measures may serve as tools for determining risk status. After students are designated as being at risk by the screening method, Tier 1 serves as preventive instruction conducted in general education classrooms. Although progress-monitoring data may be collected for all students in the classroom, some RTI models collect progress-monitoring data in this tier only for those students who are designated as at risk. The classroom teacher implements research-validated instructional practices and monitors student progress for a specified period of time, such as 5 to 10 weeks. If progress-monitoring data are collected at least every month with all students in class, these data can also serve as a gauge for determining the overall effectiveness of classroom instruction. For example, if student progress is poor for most students in the class, then the teacher may need support in implementing more effective instruction. If, however, most students are progressing well and only a subset of students show poor progress, then the assumption is made that the instructional practice is generally effective but is not working as anticipated for the subset of students. For students designated as at risk, progress-monitoring data illustrate how well they are responding to otherwise effective instruction. If student progress is poor, then other instructional practices may be tried as part of the general curriculum with progress monitoring continuing, or the student may be referred for Tier 2 preventive instruction.

General Description of Tier 2

Typically considered a part of preventive instruction or early intervening services within general education, Tier 2 instruction may be conducted by a general classroom teacher, reading specialist, school psychologist, or trained paraprofessional. Instruction at this level is considered more intensive than Tier 1 instruction because it is focused on areas of demonstrated need. For example, if students perform poorly in phonemic awareness, then Tier 2 instruction may provide a supplemental program emphasizing sounds in language. Tier 2 instruction is provided to students in small groups (e.g., 4–6 students) who perform similarly. Tier 2 instruction is made available in addition to Tier 1 instruction and may be provided several times per week for 30 or more min or as frequently as daily. This additional instruction may follow standard procedures for a particular intervention program or a student support team may devise intervention methods for groups of students. Progress monitoring for the students in Tier 2 continues for a specified period of time, such as 8 to 12 weeks, and data are used to determine whether (a) progress is good and the student returns to Tier 1 instruction, (b) progress does not occur at the expected rate and the student continues with another Tier 2 intervention, or (c) progress is poor and the student is referred to a more intensive level of instruction in Tier 3.

General Description of Tier 3

The third tier of instruction is considered to be the most intensive and is focused on individual student need. Instructional sessions may be lengthier than what is typically provided in Tier 2, instruction may be delivered one on one or to very small groups of students (e.g., 1–3 students), and the intervention program may be implemented across a longer period of time. Because students who are considered candidates for Tier 3 already have demonstrated poor performance and academic unresponsiveness to high-quality instruction as indicated by poor patterns of growth in both general education classrooms and during more focused supplemental instruction, Tier 3 intervention is developed to address specific individual needs. Although some RTI models provide this intensive level of instruction prior to special education referral, implementation of instruction at this level of intensity and specificity may overtax general education resources. The hallmark of special education has been the individualization of instruction. Consequently, the RTI model in this article utilizes Tier 3 services as special education including (a) instruction planned according to student needs, (b) development of measurable annual goals, (c) progress-monitoring data used to inform instructional decision making, and (d) special educators trained to work with students with disabilities typically delivering instruction.

In the following section, a hypothetical case study illustrates one school's RTI approach in providing effective educational services to all students. This scenario highlights the use of progress-monitoring data in identifying a young student with SLD. Ruby Sue is a first grader who differs markedly from her peers in both level of performance and rate of progress. This dual discrepancy (L. S. Fuchs & Fuchs, 1998) is used as the rationale for providing her with increasing levels of instructional support. When she repeatedly fails to respond adequately to effective classroom and supplemental instruction, a multidisciplinary team finds that she is eligible for special education and labels her as having an SLD. This case study details the use of progress-monitoring data for developing Ruby Sue's IEP goal, evaluating her response to instruction, and formatively devising effective instruction. These data are used as well to judge when Ruby Sue is successful and may be able to thrive academically without such intensive intervention.

RTI SCENARIO

Ruby Sue moved to a southeastern school district at the beginning of first grade. Johnson Elementary currently uses the Dynamic Indicators of Basic Early Literacy Skills (DIBELS; see Good & Kaminski, 2003) as a schoolwide progressive benchmark system to evaluate reading skills several times across the year for all students in the school, kindergarten through Grade 5. Given three times a year, benchmark scores indicate risk status (i.e., at risk, at some risk, or at low risk) for meeting the next benchmark. Alternate forms of DIBELS measures are available for more frequent progress monitoring.

Prior to second grade, several measures are administered at each benchmark period to evaluate a different dimension of early literacy skills. However, once students are reading connected text, oral reading fluency is the predominant measure used to gauge overall reading achievement. Oral reading fluency has been used with success for years as a part of curriculum-based measurement procedures (CBM; Deno, 1985) in monitoring the overall reading progress of students with disabilities. CBM is a research-validated form of progress monitoring and has contributed to improved student achievement when teachers use the data for instructional decision making (for review, see Stecker, Fuchs, & Fuchs, 2005).

During the 3rd week of school, all first grade students were screened on letter name fluency (i.e., naming letters of the alphabet in 1 min), phoneme segmentation fluency (i.e., producing sound segments for words provided orally), and nonsense word fluency (reading vowel–consonant or conso-nant–vowel–consonant patterns as entire "words" or as individual sounds; see Good & Kaminski, 2003 for specific information on benchmark scores and categories of risk status). Ruby Sue's scores indicated that she was at low risk on letter naming, that she had emerging skill in phonemic segmentation but was not yet established, and that she was at risk on nonsense word fluency. Mr. Dalton, the first-grade teacher, was concerned about Ruby Sue's perform-ance. Johnson Elementary provides parents with an explanation of the eval-uation system used in reading each year, so Ruby Sue's scores were sent home to her parents.

Tier 1

Because nonsense word fluency is the most sophisticated of the literacy meas-ures given early in first grade and because Ruby Sue had performed so poorly on this measure, Mr. Dalton decided to continue monitoring Ruby Sue's progress weekly on nonsense word fluency. He used the district's core reading program, which followed a code-emphasis approach. Oral activities supported vocabulary and comprehension development. Mr. Dalton provided a descrip-tion of his instruction on his school Web page. He monitored Ruby Sue's progress for 8 weeks on nonsense word fluency and sent home a copy of her progress-monitoring chart every few weeks.

After 8 weeks, Mr. Dalton met with the school's Student Support Team to discuss Ruby Sue's lack of progress. The first phase in Figure 1 shows progress-monitoring data for nonsense words during Tier 1 instruction. Ruby Sue's scores grew minimally from 7 to 11, or about 0.5 letter sounds per week on average. She fell significantly behind her peers who generally were responding well to Mr. Dalton's instruction. The Student Support Team rec-ommended that Ruby Sue enter Tier 2 supplemental instruction. Mr. Dalton sent home a note explaining this recommendation and invited Ruby Sue's parents to a conference to discuss this next step.

Tier 2

First Phase. Ruby Sue entered Tier 2 with five other children. Ms. Cortez, a reading specialist, served as the intervention teacher and provided 30 min of supplemental instruction 3 days per week in phonemic awareness and phon-ics activities according to a prescribed sequence for 10 weeks. Ms. Cortez continued to monitor Ruby Sue's progress weekly on the nonsense word flu-ency task. About every month, she also checked performance on phonemic segmentation. Ruby Sue's performance increased a little on phonemic

Figure 1. Ruby Sue's Progress Monitoring Graph for Tiers 1 and 2

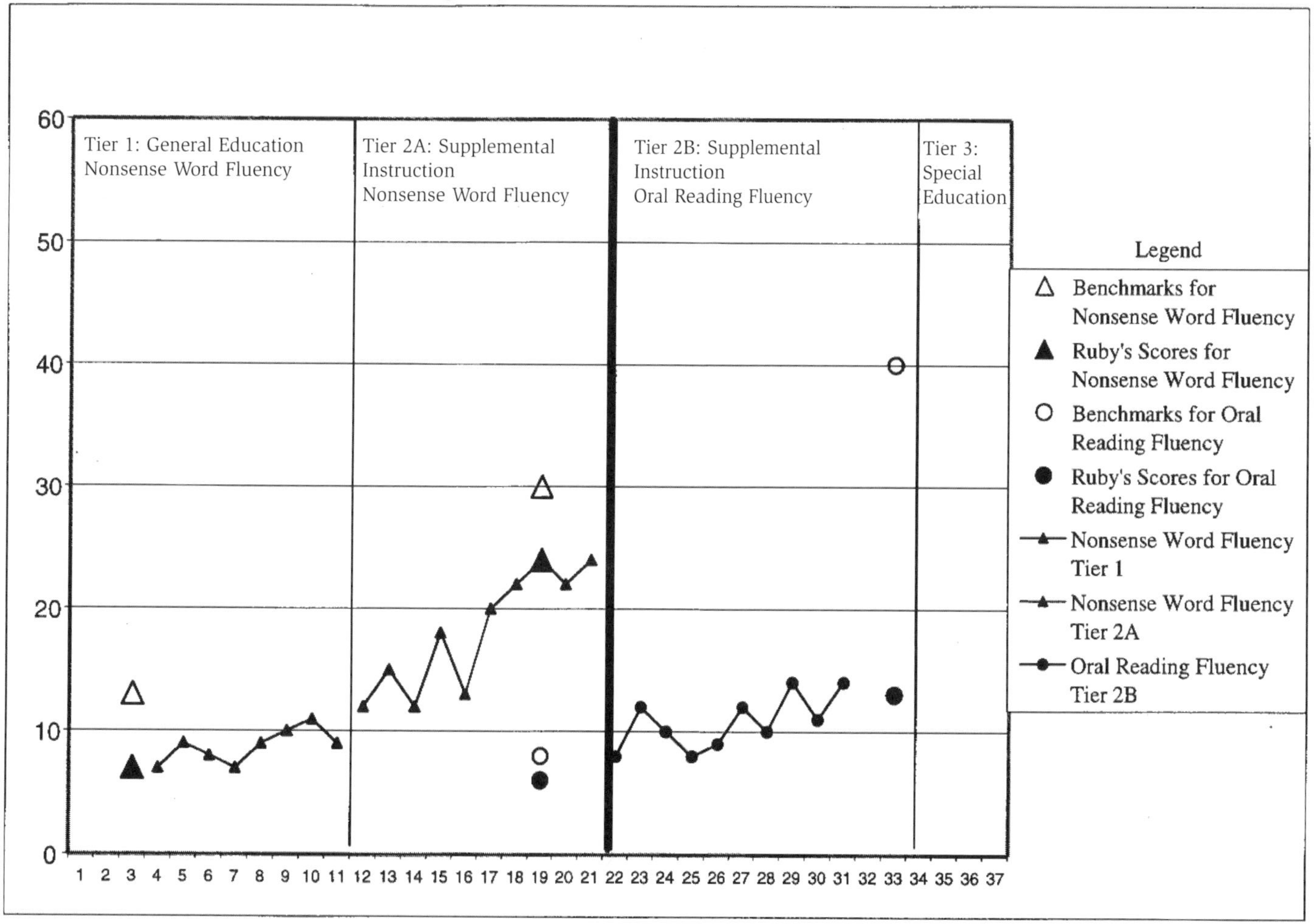

70

segmentation, and nonsense word fluency grew steadily but at a minimal level over time. Both the level of performance and the rate of improvement were less than anticipated. In addition, the winter benchmark period for DIBELS occurred during this intervention phase. Oral reading fluency was added as a measure and letter naming was dropped. Ruby Sue's score on phonemic segmentation fell just at the established level, but her nonsense word fluency score of 24 remained in the at-risk range. On the oral reading fluency measure on first-grade passages, Ruby Sue read six words correctly, in 1 min, which also fell in the at-risk range. Even with her improvement on nonsense word fluency, she still was lagging far behind her peers. Consequently, the Student Support Team decided Ruby Sue should enter a second cycle of Tier 2 preventive instruction. Figure 1 depicts the progress-monitoring data collected during this phase of supplemental instruction.

Second Phase. Ruby Sue met with 3 other students 5 days per week for 30 min during this second phase of Tier 2 instruction. Consequently, instruction in this phase was offered more frequently and with fewer students than during the first phase of Tier 2 instruction. Ms. Cortez addressed similar skills, but she spent more time modeling and providing practice opportunities with skills just demonstrated. Because oral reading fluency was the most robust of the DIBELS measures given for the rest of first grade and because that measure would continue to be used in second grade, Ms. Cortez switched to monitoring Ruby Sue's progress weekly with oral reading fluency and checked nonsense word fluency only periodically. At the end of 10 weeks, the Student Support Team met to review Ruby Sue's progress. Refer to Figure 1 for Ruby Sue's progress-monitoring data on oral reading fluency.

Ruby Sue read very slowly with 14 words correct per min at the end of this instructional phase. Her teachers reported that Ruby Sue could say sounds for about two thirds of the consonants but had difficulty blending sounds to read words. She also had a limited sight word vocabulary. However, she did appear to comprehend information adequately while listening to stories being read or during group discussion. Her very weak performance with basic reading skills, however, concerned her teachers and triggered a referral for Tier 3 intervention.

Because Ruby Sue's parents had been informed all along of Ruby Sue's progress (or lack thereof) during first grade, they were not surprised when the school recommended that Ruby Sue receive more intensive instruction and be evaluated for a possible SLD. With parental consent, a comprehensive evaluation was conducted at this point. Several assessments and rating scales were administered to rule out possible vision and hearing problems, cognitive disability, and emotional–behavioral disability. Likewise, speech–language disability and cultural and linguistic factors were eliminated as possible contributing factors to Ruby Sue's learning problems. Performance information from Ruby Sue's teachers and progress-monitoring data that demonstrated continued nonresponsiveness to otherwise effective reading instruction provided a large part of Ruby Sue's achievement data. Districts, however, may elect to conduct a more thorough investigation of a student's academic and cognitive functioning at this point (see Batsche, Kavale, & Kovaleski, 2006, for discussion). The multidisciplinary team determined that Ruby Sue had an SLD in basic reading skills and was in need of specialized services. The IEP team met to develop a long-range plan for individualized instruction. Special education services were delivered as Tier 3 intervention.

Tier 3

IEP Goal Development. The IEP team needed to develop a year-long goal in reading for Ruby Sue for near the end of her second-grade year. Although they had data on oral reading fluency for first-grade measures, they gathered baseline data on second-grade passages as well. Ruby Sue's average score on two second-grade passages was 12 words correct per min, which fell close to her scores on first-grade passages. She seemed to read the same words across all the passages. The team knew that oral reading fluency was a technically sound measure for monitoring overall reading achievement in elementary students and chose to use this measure for developing Ruby Sue's IEP goal. Because the team thought that the gap existing between her peers' and her performance could be closed with intensive, specialized instruction, the IEP team set 90 words correct per min as her annual goal to be achieved by Week 34 of second grade for Ruby Sue. The team considered several factors in setting this long-range goal. First, 90 words correct per min was the DIBELS benchmark for the lowest score that still fell in the low-risk category by the end of second grade. Second, the team looked at average and ambitious rates of growth for second graders (see L. S. Fuchs, Fuchs, Hamlett, Walz, & Germann, 1993). Realistic and ambitious rates of growth per week were 1.5 and 2 words correct, respectively, at second grade. Approximately 37 instructional weeks (i.e., 4 weeks left in first grade and 33 weeks in second grade) would occur before the date of the annual goal. A particular weekly growth rate could be multiplied by the total number of instructional weeks left to meet the goal and then could be added to baseline performance to determine a reasonable goal. In Ruby Sue's case, an ambitious growth rate of 2 words per week multiplied by 37 weeks was 74 words. Then, the 74 words were added to the baseline of 11 words to yield a goal of 85 words correct per minute, which also could be rounded up to 90. Ruby Sue's parents wanted her to be able to read like her peers and supported the provision of intensive services so Ruby Sue could get the specialized help she needed to reduce her gap in performance. Thus, the IEP team designated 90 words correct per min in second-grade passages as the long-term goal. Ruby Sue's IEP statements for current level of performance and her annual goal are listed below.

- *Current Level of Performance:* Given passages written at the second-grade level, Ruby Sue currently reads aloud 11 words correct in 1 min.

Figure 2. Ruby Sue's Individualized Education Program (IEP) Progress Monitoring Graph

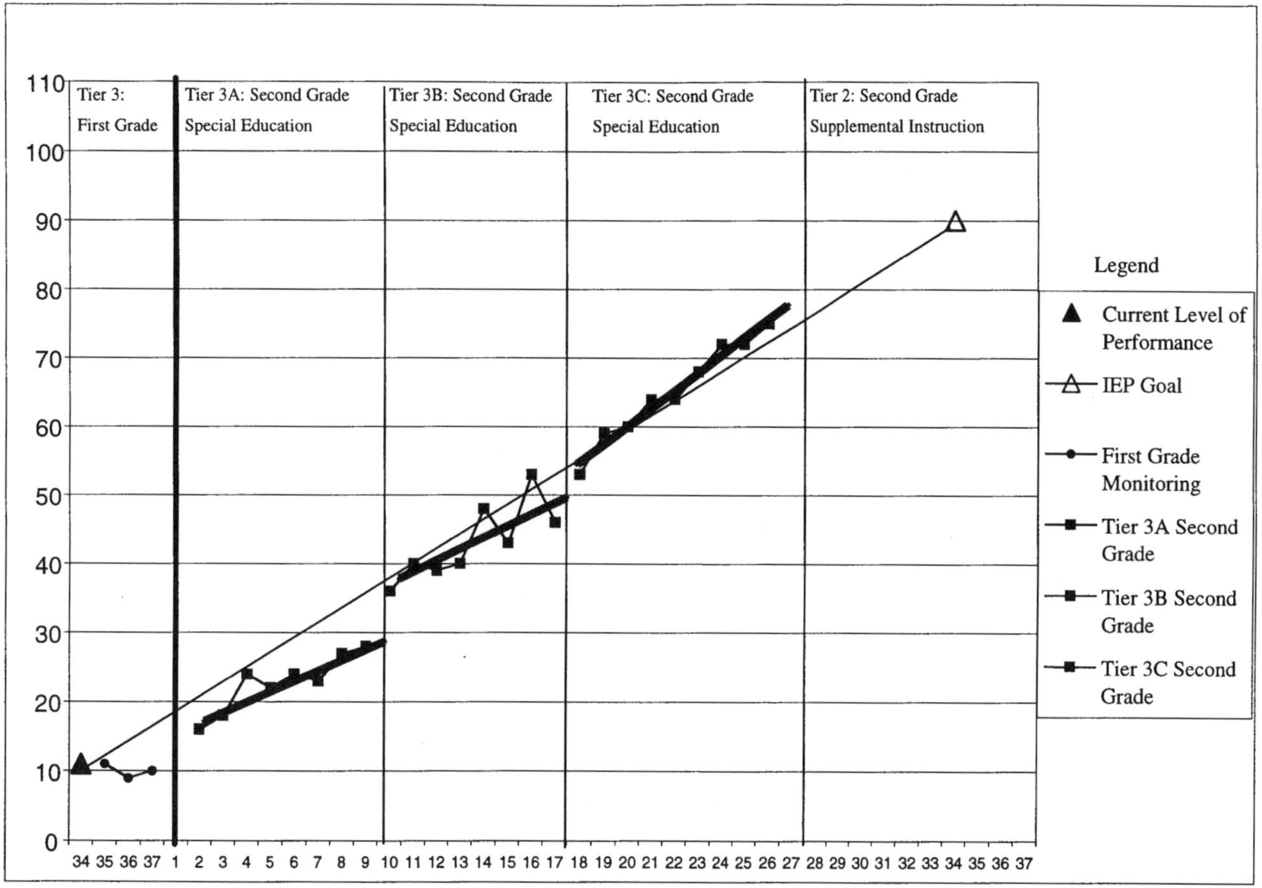

- *Annual Goal:* Given passages written at the second-grade level, Ruby Sue will read aloud at least 90 words correct per min in 37 weeks.

Instructional Decision Making. Figure 2 shows Ruby Sue's IEP progress-monitoring graph. The dark triangle represents Ruby Sue's baseline performance on oral reading fluency in second-grade passages at Week 34 of her first grade. The open triangle depicts the long-term goal set for Week 34 of Ruby Sue's second-grade year. The line connecting baseline and the goal is the goal line, which depicts how quickly Ruby Sue needs to progress through the curriculum in order to meet her annual goal. Ruby Sue's teachers continued to monitor her progress frequently and compared her actual rate of improvement periodically against the goal line to judge whether Ruby Sue was making adequate progress toward attaining her long-term goal. When Ruby Sue appeared to be making less growth than anticipated, her teacher modified instruction in some way to try to stimulate better achievement. When Ruby Sue made progress that was better than anticipated, the team raised her goal and considered whether a trial of less intensive instruction, such as that provided in Tier 2, was warranted. Thus, progress-monitoring data were used within an RTI model as an objective basis for determining when modifications were necessary within instructional tiers and when movement in and out of instructional tiers appeared justified.

Instructional Implementation. Ms. Ames, the special educator, worked with Ruby Sue, along with 2 other students, for 75 min daily on literacy activities specific to Ruby Sue's needs. This instruction occurred in addition to Ruby Sue's core reading program and focused heavily on decoding skills, including letter–sound correspondences for consonants and short vowels, blending to sound out words, high-frequency sight words, and use of word lists and teacher-made passages for reading practice. Although some oral activities supported vocabulary and comprehension, the greatest proportion of time was spent helping Ruby Sue to read words and connect text independently. Although Ms. Ames primarily used first-grade materials for instruction, she continued to assess Ruby Sue's oral reading fluency on second-grade passages. The trend line, or slope, through the first instructional phase of 8 weeks in second grade illustrates increasing progress but not quite at the desired rate when compared to the goal line (refer to Figure 2 and the superimposed trend line on the Tier 3A data set). Therefore, Ms. Ames made an instructional enhancement to her program by adding more sight words, teaching sound correspondences for common letter combinations, and using decodable books for reading practice. She had Ruby Sue spell and write the words she was reading. By examining the progress-monitoring data for the next phase of instruction of 8 weeks, Ms. Ames could see that Ruby Sue continued to improve. She had two scores that actually fell above the goal line; however, the overall trend of Ruby Sue's performance was a little less steep than the goal line.

Consequently, Ms. Ames sought to improve Ruby Sue's rate of growth once again. Ms. Ames considered Ruby Sue's performance and the aspects of the program that could be modified to better meet Ruby Sue's needs. Because Ruby Sue was making good improvement, Ms. Ames continued with her general plan for decoding instruction but added fluency-building activities and expanded her repertoire of reading selections. She primarily used second-grade materials at this point, and they also reread passages used in the core program earlier in the year. Ms. Ames previewed vocabulary and skills for upcoming lessons in the general classroom.

In this way, Ms. Ames used progress-monitoring data to determine the relative effectiveness of her instructional procedures. Periodically, she examined the actual rate of Ruby Sue's progress against the anticipated rate of progress to judge how well the instructional program was working for Ruby Sue. Over time, she was able to construct more effective instruction for Ruby Sue by introducing program modifications to better suit Ruby Sue's needs.

Movement Among Tiers. Looking at progress-monitoring data for the third phase of instruction revealed that Ruby Sue had made substantial progress. Ruby Sue's trend of performance actually exceeded the anticipated rate of growth depicted by the goal line. If Ruby Sue continued in this fashion, she likely would exceed her annual goal. Ms. Ames met with the IEP team to discuss Ruby Sue's progress. The team decided that Ruby Sue's goal should be raised to 105 words correct per min and that a cycle of Tier 2 instruction should be conducted without Tier 3 intensive intervention. Progress monitoring would continue. If Ruby Sue were to continue to progress well, Tier 2 instruction may be continued for the rest of the year. If Ruby Sue's progress-monitoring data showed little progress or a decline, more intensive Tier 3 intervention would again be considered. In this way, progress-monitoring data could be used to monitor Ruby Sue's responsiveness to instruction but also could be used to judge the overall effectiveness of the instructional program for Ruby Sue. Progress-monitoring data could be used to track movement in and out of instructional tiers.

In Ruby Sue's case, the IEP team did not release her fully from special education. Her instructional placement changed to Tier 2 services, and supplemental instructional time was reduced to 30 min. However, the special educator continued to monitor Ruby Sue's progress toward her IEP goal and to consult with the Tier 2 intervention teacher regarding instructional practices. Progress-monitoring data were used to direct the level of intensity of instructional support she needed. Movement in and out of instructional tiers was flexible, with special and general education services working in a coordinated fashion. Once Ruby Sue demonstrated a positive growth trajectory without intensive special education provided in Tier 3, the IEP team could dismiss her entirely from special education supervision.

REMAINING QUESTIONS AND CHALLENGES FOR RTI IMPLEMENTATION

As has been discussed in this series, advantages of using an RTI approach to schoolwide assessment and instructional practices are many. Reconfiguring school resources to assist students at different levels of instructional intensity establishes a system of educational service for all students in need before they experience a lengthy cycle of failure. Early intervening services may ultimately reduce the number of students referred for special education or may reduce the impact of a disability on students' academic progress. Emphasizing the use of evidence-based practices at all instructional levels contributes to student success and may eliminate or reduce ineffective instruction as a cause of poor student performance. Progress-monitoring data can be used as an objective source of information for judging student achievement, evaluating instructional efficacy, and planning instruction. For example, progress-monitoring data can be used to develop instructional programs formatively to accelerate student progress. Movement of individual students among instructional tiers is flexible and is based on student data and research-based criteria for likelihood of success.

With RTI practices, however, several issues remain to be resolved. Central to the use of data generated through RTI for potential SLD identification is the concern over actual implementation of evidence-based instructional practices. If the expectation holds true that RTI practices eliminate students from special education referral whose low performance is primarily due to ineffective instruction, then RTI models must verify that evidence-based practices are in place in primary and secondary prevention programs. Consequently, schools are compelled to consider the resources that are necessary for supporting high-quality instruction in all levels of instructional practice.

If progress-monitoring data are used to capture overall student response to instruction, then progress-monitoring measures must be technically sound, and research evidence should guide the use of these data for decision making. For IEP development, goals should be written that are measurable and for which suitable progress-monitoring measures can be used to judge the adequacy of student progress toward ultimately attaining them. Consequently, it may be advantageous to select a measure that can be used for progress monitoring across the entire year. With Ruby Sue, different tools were selected for monitoring her progress across the first grade. Having one tool, such as word identification fluency (see L. S. Fuchs, Fuchs, & Compton, 2004) in first grade (or letter–sound fluency in kindergarten) for monitoring growth across the entire year may aid in decision making and be an important consideration when selecting measures for monitoring IEP goals in early grade levels.

Other technical questions relate to the number of tiers included in the RTI model, length and number of preventive treatment phases within each tier, frequency of progress monitoring (e.g., once or twice per week), and comprehensiveness of special education evaluation (for discussion, see Fletcher,

2006; L. S. Fuchs & Fuchs, 2006). Other issues include the movement in and out of tiers. For example, how long should a child remain in intensive special education services? What procedures should be followed when a student performs well in a more intensive instructional tier but performs poorly when moved to a less intensive tier?

Although some RTI work has been done with respect to mathematics, most RTI models to date have addressed reading with young, elementary-age students. How can RTI be implemented effectively across subjects and grade levels? What measures should be used with older students who may be in need of special education services? As RTI holds much promise for improved instruction and better alignment and collaboration between general and special education, continued research is needed to guide the adoption of specific RTI practices by states and districts.

REFERENCES

Batsche, G. M., Kavale, K., A., & Kovaleski, J. F. (2006). Competing views: A dialogue on response to intervention. *Assessment for Effective Intervention, 32*(1), 6–19.

Deno, S. L. (1985). Curriculum-based measurement: The emerging alternative. *Exceptional Children, 52*, 219–232.

Fletcher, J. M. (2006). The need for response to instruction models of learning disabilities. *Perspectives, 32*(1), 12–15.

Fuchs, D., Mock, D., Morgan, P., & Young, C. L. (2003). Responsiveness-to-intervention: Definitions, evidence, and implication for the learning disabilities construct. *Learning Disabilities Research and Practice, 18*(3), 157–171.

Fuchs, L. S., & Fuchs, D. (1998). Treatment validity: A unifying concept for reconceptualizing the identification of learning disabilities. *Learning Disabilities Research and Practice, 13*, 204–219.

Fuchs, L. S., & Fuchs, D. (2006). Identifying learning disabilities with RTI. *Perspectives, 32*(1), 39–43.

Fuchs, L. S., Fuchs, D., & Compton, D. L. (2004). Monitoring early reading development in first grade: Word identification fluency versus nonsense word fluency. *Exceptional Children, 71*, 7–21.

Fuchs, L. S., Fuchs, D., Hamlett, C. L., Walz, L., & Germann, G. (1993). Formative evaluation of academic progress: How much growth can we expect? *School Psychology Review, 22*, 27–48.

Good, R. H. III, & Kaminski, R. A. (2003). *Dynamic indicators of basic early literacy skills* (6th ed.). Longmont, CO: Sopris West. Also available at: *http://dibels. uoregon.edu*

Marston, D., Muyskens, P., Lau, M., & Canter, A. (2003). Problem-solving model for decision making with high-incidence disabilities: The Minneapolis experience. *Learning Disabilities Research and Practice, 18*, 187–200.

Stecker, P. M., Fuchs, L. S., & Fuchs, D. (2005). Using curriculum-based measurement to improve student achievement: Review of research. *Psychology in the Schools, 42*, 795–819.

Tilly, W. D. (2006). Diagnosing the learning enabled: The promise of response to intervention. *Perspectives, 32*(1), 20–24.

Vaughn, S., & Chard, D. (2006). Three-tier intervention research studies: Description of two related projects. *Perspectives, 32*(1), 30–34.

Originally published in *TEACHING Exceptional Children,* Vol. 39, No. 5, pp. 50–57.

8

Dynamic Assessment as Responsiveness to Intervention: A Scripted Protocol to Identify Young At-Risk Readers

Douglas Fuchs, Lynn S. Fuchs, Donald L. Compton,
Bobette Bouton, Erin Caffrey, and Lisa Hill

RESPONSIVENESS TO INSTRUCTION: "INSTRUCTION" IS THE TEST

Many teachers, administrators, and policy makers are currently discussing Responsiveness to Intervention (RTI) as a method of providing both early intervention to at-risk learners and more valid identification of children with learning disabilities (LD). RTI is viewed by many stakeholders as more valid than traditional methods of identification because it guarantees in principle that all children participate in scientifically validated curriculum and instruction. Hence, practitioners working within an RTI framework are expected to reduce the likelihood that untaught or poorly taught nondisabled students are misidentified as disabled. With classroom teachers using scientifically validated curricula and instruction, all children, or at least most children, should get the education they need without having to "wait to fail" when RTI is implemented well.

RTI as a method of disability identification has been legitimized in the recently reauthorized Individuals with Disabilities Education Improvement Act of 2004 and in accompanying Regulations that were released in August 2006. The Regulations prohibit states from requiring use of IQ-achievement discrepancy, and they encourage implementation of RTI (cf. Yell, Shriner, & Katsiyannis, 2006).

The essence of RTI as a method of disability identification is that instruction becomes the "test"—as much a test as the Wide Range Achievement Test or Stanford-Binet. In other words, instruction is the test stimulus and the student's level or rate of performance is her response. Just as commercial publishers, such professional groups as the American Psychological Association, examiners, and others worry about the validity of *test instruments,* practitioners using RTI need to be concerned about the validity of their instruction. Choosing scientifically validated curricula and academic programs that address at-risk students' needs and implementing them with fidelity are necessary to ensure the validity of the RTI process. If practitioners choose invalid or unvalidated instructional programs or implement validated instructional programs without fidelity, a child's nonresponsiveness can become impossible to interpret.

Current operationalizations of RTI vary considerably. Some define RTI in terms of five tiers; others, four or three tiers. There are advocates of a "problem solving" approach to instruction and, alternatively, proponents of standard treatment protocols. A few insist special education should be excluded from the tier structure; others insist on its inclusion. Those disagreements notwithstanding, we find general agreement that within an RTI framework, instruction should become increasingly intensive as a student moves from lower to higher tiers. We find consensus, too, that movement from one tier to the next should be predicated on a student's unresponsiveness to instruction. The more chronic the student's unresponsiveness, the higher she moves through the tier structure.

At least two widely acknowledged concerns with RTI's tier structure arise. First, because instruction at each tier may last 8 to 10 weeks, a chronically unresponsive child could possibly fail across multiple tiers for 30 weeks or more before practitioners recognize that she requires special education. Second, usually an explicit expectation is held that the instruction at Tier 2 (and at higher tiers) is expertly delivered. Where this expertise will come from is unclear. Those concerns lead to this question: Might an easier-to-implement and more efficient RTI be possible—one that is more feasible to scale up and that identifies sooner the nonresponders in need of more intensive instruction? This question brings us to a discussion of dynamic assessment (DA).

A MORE EFFICIENT RTI?

DA Versus Traditional Tests. An important concern about the use of many traditional one-point-in-time tests with low-achieving, young students is that they do not predict future academic performance very accurately. This inaccuracy is partly because of so-called "floor effects." That is, many unskilled kindergartners and first graders obtain a score of zero when administered a traditional reading test such as the Word Identification subtest of the Woodcock Reading Mastery Tests. This score of zero can reflect at least two important limitations of many traditional tests. One, many do a poor job of sampling (i.e., devoting too few items to) basic or elementary skills. Two, they typically assess only two states: unaided success or failure. From a Vygotskian perspective, however, children may be somewhere between those two states: unable to perform the task independently but able to achieve success with minimal assistance. DA can help one explore the amount and nature of this minimal assistance. Thus, it is an index of a child's readiness to change and, as such, represents a unique means of differentiating performance among children at the low end of the achievement continuum (e.g., Campione & Brown, 1987; Spector, 1992).

DA has been described as the assessment of learning potential (e.g., Budoff, Gimon, & Corman, 1974; Budoff, Meskin, & Harrison, 1971); mediated learning (e.g., Feuerstein, Rand, & Hoffman, 1979); testing-the-limits (Carlson & Wiedel, 1978, 1979); mediated assessment (e.g., Bransford, Delclos, Vye, Burns, & Hasselbring, 1987); and assisted learning and transfer by graduated prompts (e.g., Campione, Brown, Ferrara, Jones, & Steinberg, 1985). Across its variants, DA differs from traditional testing in terms of the nature of the examiner-student relationship, the content of feedback, and the emphasis on process rather than product (Grigorenko & Sternberg, 1998).

In traditional testing, the examiner is a neutral or "objective" participant who provides standardized directions but not, typically, performance-contingent feedback. Many DA examiners, by contrast, not only give performance-contingent feedback but also offer instruction in response to student failure to alter or enhance the student's performance. Put differently, traditional testing is oriented toward the product (i.e., level of performance) of student learning, whereas the DA examiner's interest is both in the product and in the process (i.e., rate of growth) of the learning.

Some claim that DA's dual focus on the level and rate of learning makes it a better predictor of future performance. Consider the child who enters kindergarten with little background knowledge. He scores poorly on traditional tests but, during DA, he demonstrates maturity, attention, and motivation and, more importantly, learns a task—or a series of tasks—with only a modest amount of guidance from the examiner. Because of this ability, he is seen as being in less danger of school failure than his classmates who are scoring poorly on both traditional tests and DA.

Therefore, DA may help decrease the number of "false positives," or children who seem at risk but who, with timely instruction, may respond relatively quickly and perform within acceptable limits. Data from DA may also help identify the type and intensity of intervention necessary for academic success. DA incorporates a test-teach-test format, conceptually similar to RTI techniques. However, DA can potentially measure one's responsiveness within a much shorter time frame. More about this aspect is discussed later.

DA's Predictive Validity. Few proponents of DA say, "Substitute it for traditional tests." Rather, we believe, many would claim it should be used in conjunction with, or as a supplement to, traditional tests (e.g., Lidz, 1987). Notwithstanding such enthusiasm for DA, infrequent research has been conducted on its psychometric properties (see Grigorenko & Sternberg, 1998, and Swanson, 2001, for reviews); even less on its predictive validity. Recently, Caffrey, Fuchs, and Fuchs (in press) conducted a review of this small body of extant research, exploring DA's predictive validity. Results indicated that traditional tests and DA similarly predicted future academic performance, irrespective of student type (e.g., normally achieving children versus at-risk children). However, findings also suggested that DA taps achievement differently than traditional achievement tests and cognitive tests and explains significant and unique variance in the prediction of students' general reasoning, verbal achievement, and mathematics achievement. Caffrey and colleagues' review also determined that DA predicted achievement more accurately (a) when examiner feedback was noncontingent on student performance; (b) when examinees were students with disabilities rather than normally achieving children; and (c) when achievement was defined as DA posttests and criterion-referenced tests instead of norm-referenced tests and teachers' judgment about student performance.

Purpose of This Article

Prediction of future achievement is important because it can identify students who are at risk for school failure and in need of more intensive intervention. Students enter school with different cognitive strengths and weaknesses, different home and community experiences and expectations, and different levels of prior education. Those capacities, experiences, and expectations result in various levels of academic competence and readiness. Traditional testing mostly reflects what a child currently knows; it does not clearly indicate learning potential. DA, in conjunction with traditional testing, may indicate more accurately a student's potential for change, likeliness of school success, and appropriate instruction.

Partly on the basis of results from the review by Caffrey and colleagues (in press), we set out to develop a DA measure in early reading, hoping that it might eventually prove useful to practitioners who wish to identify nonresponders to classroom (Tier 1) instruction more quickly than they can achieve with many current RTI approaches. Toward that end, we conducted two studies—a short-term pilot study and a longer study. In both, children in late fall of their first-grade year were administered a battery of traditional tests and a DA measure that focused on early reading skills. For the next 5 weeks in the pilot study and 11 weeks in the longer study, the children participated in reading instruction, during which their progress was monitored weekly. In each study, we explored whether our DA measure—apart from the battery of traditional tests—had value in predicting children's performance (across the 5 weeks in the pilot study and 11 weeks in the longer study). The primary purpose of this article is to describe and share a portion of our early reading DA measure. After describing it, we comment briefly on findings from the larger of the two evaluations.

DA PROTOCOL TO IDENTIFY AT-RISK STUDENTS

General Directions

Our DA measure consists of nonwords separated into three subtests: CVC, CVCe, and Doubling (Fuchs, Fuchs, & Compton, 2005; see Figure 1 for the script that directs the administration of the CVC segment of the DA measure). All nonwords have either a short "o" or long "o" vowel sound. In each subtest, students are given five opportunities to master the content (criterion is 5 of 6 correct). If students fail to master the content at the first opportunity (Level 1), they are given a hint to help them learn the decoding rule (i.e., CVC, CVCe, or Doubling). If students fail to master the content at the second opportunity (Level 2), they are given a more explicit hint. Increasingly explicit hints are given until the student reaches mastery (5 of 6 correct) or until all hints have been administered (Level 5). If students do not reach mastery by Level 5 of the CVC subtest, the CVCe and Doubling subtests are not administered. Similarly, if students do not reach mastery on the CVCe subtest, the Doubling subtest is not administered. Each subtest is scored 1 through 5. A score of 1 indicates that a student reached mastery at the first opportunity (Level 1); a score of 5 indicates that a student reached mastery at the fifth and final opportunity (Level 5). If students are not administered a subtest (owing to lack of mastery of lower content), they are automatically given a score of 5. The scores of the three subtests are added for a total score. A lower score indicates quicker mastery of content.

Subtests

CVC. In the CVC subtest, the test items at each level are *fot, gop, vop, wot, jop,* and *zot.*

- *Level 1: Reading to the Child* includes modeling the reading of nonsense words with the short "o" sound (not the test items).
- *Level 2: Teaching Onset* instructs the student to attend to the first sound of each nonsense word.
- *Level 3: Teaching Rime* instructs the student to attend to the last two sounds of each word.
- *Level 4: Teaching Onset-Rime Blending I* instructs the student to decode the onset and rime separately and then to blend them together into a word.
- *Level 5: Teaching Onset-Rime Blending II* teaches the same content as Level 4.

CVCe. In the CVCe subtest, the test items at each level are *fote, gope, vope, wote, jope,* and *zote.*

- *Level I: Reading to the Child* includes modeling reading of nonsense words with the long "o" sound (not the test items).

Figure 1. CVC Script

Level 1: Reading to the Child

I'm going to read some words. These are nonsense words. Not real words. See if you can figure out what these nonsense words say. I'll read them first.

(Point to each word as you read.)

bod . . . . . . zod
bom . . . . . zom

> **Now you read these nonsense words:**
>
> fot, gop, vop, wot, jop, zot

Level 2: Teaching Onset

These words are also nonsense words. I'm going to read them and put them in two piles. Over here *(point)* I'll put the words that start with the letter "z." The letter "z" says /z/. Here *(point)*, I'll put the words that begin with the letter "b," /b/. Watch me.

(Sort the word cards by first reading the card, then placing it correctly into one of the two piles. When you've sorted all the cards, reshuffle them and place the deck in front of the child and tell the child.)

Now you make two piles. One pile is for words that begin with "z." The other pile is for words that begin with "b."

(Read each card aloud and then give it to the child, helping the child if necessary to place it in the correct location.)

> **Now, read these nonsense words:**
>
> fot, gop, vop, wot, jop, zot

Level 3: Teaching Rime

These cards also have nonsense words. Just like before, I'll read them and make two piles. But now I'm going to look at the **last two** letters of each word.

(Show the card with bom on it. Indicate that the last 2 letters are underlined. Show another card with bod on it. Again, the last 2 letters are underlined.)

Here *(point)*, I'll put the words that end in "o-m." O-m says /om/. Here *(point)* I'll put words that end in "o-d," /od/. Here. *(point)* Watch me do this.

(Sort the cards by first reading each one. Then place each card correctly into one of the two piles.)

Now you make two piles. One pile is for words that end in /od/. The other pile is for words that end in /om./

> **Now you read these nonsense words:**
>
> fot, gop, vop, wot, jop, zot

continues

Figure 1. *Continued*

Level 4: Teaching Onset-Rime Blending I

(One example, no student practice, no feedback.)

This letter is "b"; it says /b/. These two letters ("o m") say /om/. Together the sounds say /b/ /om/ /bom/.

(Repeat with "z" and "od.")

Now you read these nonsense words:

fot, gop, vop, wot, jop, zot

Level 5: Teaching Onset-Rime Blending II

(Repeat Onset-Rime I)

This letter is "b"; it says /b/. These two letters ("o-m") say /om/. Together the sounds say /b/ /om/ /bom/.

(Repeat with "z" and "o-d.")

Now you be the teacher. You teach me how to read the word bom. I'll show you how. First, point to the "b" and say, "This says/b/. What does it say?" Your turn.

(Wait for the child to repeat. Repeat the directive if necessary. When the child completes the directive, respond as if you're the student. Then point to the "o-m" and say,)

"These letters say /om./ What do they say?" Your turn.

(Wait for the child to repeat. Help the child as necessary, and then respond as if you're the student.)

Now say to me, these sounds say /bom/.

(Repeat with lod.)

(Give the child a card with zod, bod, mod, and zom on it. Say)

Now let's play a game called Guess My Word. I am going to say a word, and I would like you to point to that word on this card.

(Play the game using all the words once. Then you and the child switch roles. The child says a word, you point to it, and you say it.)

Now you say one of these words, and I'll point to it.

Now please read these words:

fot, gop, vop, wot, jop, zot

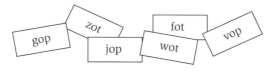

- *Level 2: Hearing Long and Short Middle Vowel Sounds* instructs the student to listen to the difference between the short "o" sound and long "o" sound in word pairs (e.g., *dod* and *dode*).

- *Level 3: Teaching "Long" and "Short" Vowel Terminology* instructs students to use the terms "long 'o'" and "short 'o'" and to recognize their visual symbols (i.e., " ō " and " ŏ").

- *Level 4: Teaching the "Magic e" Rule* instructs the student that when an "e" appears at the end of the word, the "o" says its name and makes the long "o" sound; and that when no "e" appears at the end of the word, the "o" does not say its name and makes the short "o" sound.

- *Level 5: Teaching the "Magic e" Rule With Color Emphasis* is identical to Level 4, except the "Magic e" is colored red to help the student attend to it.

Doubling. In the Doubling subtest, the test items at each level are *fotting, goping, vopping, woting, jopping,* and *zoting*. Before any of the testing levels are administered, the examiner conducts a preteaching session to make sure the student can recognize "—ing" and say its sound /ing/.

- *Level 1: Reading to the Child* includes modeling nonsense words with single and double consonants that also have the suffix —ing (not the test items).

- *Level 2: Long Versus Short Vowel Sound* instructs students to listen to the number of sounds in each word and determine whether the vowel sounds the same or different.

- *Level 3: Single Versus Double Consonant* involves the examiner's modeling words while asking students to attend to whether the word has a single or double consonant; however, no explicit rule is stated.

- *Level 4: Teaching the Doubling Rule* instructs the student that when a word has one consonant, the "o" says its name and makes the long "o" sound; and that when a word has two consonants, the "o" does not say its name and makes the short "o" sound.

- *Level 5: Teaching the Doubling Rule With Color Emphasis* is identical to Level 4 except that the consonant in each single-consonant word is colored red and the consonants in each double-consonant word are colored green to help the student attend to the difference.

EVALUATING THE DA PROTOCOL

To determine whether the DA protocol may strengthen practitioners' capacity to predict at-risk students' reading performance, we conducted two studies as part of our work at the National Research Center on Learning Disabilities. The first, in 2004 to 2005, was a pilot study that we do not discuss here. The second, conducted the following year, began with the recruitment of four schools, two high-poverty Title I schools and two non–Title I schools, in the Metro-Nashville Public Schools. In those four study schools we enlisted the help of 22 kindergarten and first-grade teachers. From their classrooms we obtained parental consents to work with 216 students.

We screened the students on phonological awareness and beginning decoding skills to ensure they would be capable of achieving at least partial success on our DA protocol. A total of 133 students (28 of 111 kindergartners and all 105 first graders) met the screening criteria and continued in the study. All were individually administered eight measures: Rapid Letter Naming (RLN), Segmentation, Woodcock Reading Mastery Tests—Revised (Word Attack; Woodcock; 1987), Wide Range Achievement Test (WRAT)-Reading, WRAT-Arithmetic (Jastak & Wilkinson, 1984), Wechsler Abbreviated Scale of Intelligence (WASI; Wechsler, 1999) Block Design, WASI-Matrix Reasoning, and CBM in reading. Well-trained examiners administered the measures in random order in one session in the students' schools. The DA protocol was individually administered in a second session.

Eleven weeks after testing, the children were tested again in the same fashion as previously, with these exceptions: We eliminated the WRAT-Arithmetic test; we used two different subtests of the WASI (Vocabulary and Similarities); and we added an oral reading fluency measure and the Wechsler Individualized Achievement Test-Spelling. Between the first and second rounds of testing, we monitored weekly each of the kindergarten and first-grade children's progress in general education so that we had 11 CBM data points in reading, using Word Identification Fluency, on every child. Hence, one might think of our effort as an intervention study with "intervention" defined as general classroom instruction.

As indicated, this study's purpose was to determine which of the various measures we administered, including the DA protocol, explained (or predicted) students' responsiveness to 11 weeks of classroom instruction. To do so, we pitted the measures against one another, looking for how well each accounted for the children's reading performance. Our primary interest here was to determine whether DA had important value added, or whether it was merely redundant with the other measures. Our analyses suggested DA was indeed a valuable explanation and predictor of end-of-11-week reading performance—even after we first used the decoding inventory, CBM slope (reading progress), and other reading measures as predictors. That is, DA seemed to tap into aspects of young children's reading performance that the other measures did not.

CONCLUSION

These preliminary findings suggest that practitioners using DA, together with a small subset of such additional measures as CBM slope, might identify young at-risk readers for Tier 2 instruction more quickly (i.e., perhaps as quickly as a couple of test sessions) than others using RTI approaches that require many weeks of Tier 1 instruction. Put differently, by calibrating student responsiveness to DA and other select measures, practitioners might be capable of selecting an appropriate level of instructional intensity for each at-risk student and initiating that instruction within days rather than weeks.

That said, many may view as improbable the suggestion that DA, in combination with a small group of additional measures, might substitute for weeks of instructional intervention as a diagnostic test of whether a student will eventually prove responsive. More probable, perhaps, is that DA may help practitioners (a) trim the number of children who enter Tier 2 instruction by eliminating so-called false positives who do not really need the more intensive (and costly) instruction, and (b) identify very needy children who will likely be unresponsive to Tier 2 instruction and should proceed, instead, to Tier 3 (special education). In the interest of encouraging such exploration by practitioners and researchers, we have provided a partial script for our DA protocol and encourage readers to modify it, or add to it, to further explore DA's possible usefulness as an alternative approach or supplement to RTI.

REFERENCES

Bransford, J. C., Delclos, J. R., Vye, N. J., Burns, M., & Hasselbring, T. S. (1987). State of the art and future directions. In C. S. Lidz (Ed.), *Dynamic assessment: An interactional approach to evaluating learning potential* (pp. 479–496). New York: Guilford Press.

Budoff, M., Gimon, A., & Corman, L. (1974). Learning potential measurement with Spanish-speaking youth as an alternative to IQ tests: A first report. *Interamerican Journal of Psychology, 8,* 233–246.

Budoff, M., Meskin, J., & Harrison, R. H. (1971). Educational test of the learning-potential hypothesis. *American Journal of Mental Deficiency, 76,* 159–169.

Caffrey, E., Fuchs, D., & Fuchs, L. S. (in press). The predictive validity of dynamic assessment: A review. *Journal of Special Education.*

Campione, J. C., & Brown, A. L. (1987). Linking dynamic assessment with school achievement. In C. S. Lidz (Ed.), *Dynamic testing* (pp. 82–115). New York: Guilford Press.

Campione, J. C., Brown, A. L., Ferrara, R. A., Jones, R. S., & Steinberg, E. (1985). Breakdowns in flexible use of information: Intelligence-related differences in transfer following equivalent learning performance. *Intelligence, 9,* 297–315.

Carlson, J. S., & Wiedel, K. H. (1978). Use of testing-the-limits procedures in the testing of intellectual capabilities in children with learning difficulties. *American Journal of Mental Deficiency, 11,* 559-564.

Carlson, J. S., & Wiedel, K. H. (1979). Toward a differential testing approach: Testing-the-limits employing the Raven matrices. *Intelligence, 3,* 323–344.

Feuerstein, R., Rand, Y., & Hoffman, M. B. (1979). *The dynamic assessment of retarded performers: The Learning Potential Assessment Device.* Baltimore: University Park Press.

Fuchs, D., Fuchs, L. S., & Compton, D. L. (2005). Dynamic assessment for young at-risk readers. Unpublished test. Nashville, TN: Vanderbilt University.

Grigorenko, E. L., & Sternberg, R. J. (1998). Dynamic testing. *Psychological Bulletin, 124,* 75–111.

Jastak, S., & Wilkinson, G. S. (1984). The Wide Range Achievement Test—Revised. Wilmington, DE: Jastak Associates.

Lidz, C. S. (1987). *Dynamic assessment: An interactional approach to evaluating learning potential.* New York: Guilford Press.

Spector, J. E. (1992). Predicting progress in beginning reading: Dynamic assessment of phonemic awareness. *Journal of Educational Psychology, 84,* 353–363.

Swanson, H. L. (2001). A selective synthesis of the experimental literature on dynamic assessment. *Review of Educational Research, 71,* 321–363.

Wechsler, D. (1999). Abbreviated Scale of Intelligence. San Antonio, TX: Psychological Corporation.

Woodcock, R. (1987). Woodcock Reading Mastery Tests—Revised. Circle Pines, MN: American Guidance Service.

Yell, M. L., Shriner, J. G., & Katsiyannis, A. (2006). Individuals With Disabilities Education Improvement Act of 2004 and IDEA Regulations of 2006: Implications for educators, administrators, and teacher trainers. *Focus on Exceptional Children, 39*(1), 1–24.

The research described in this article was conducted as part of the work of the National Research Center on Learning Disabilities and supported in part by Grant #H324U010004 from the U.S. Department of Education, Office of Special Education Programs; and Core Grant #HD15052 from the National Institute of Child Health and Human Development, both to Vanderbilt University. This work does not reflect positions or policies of these agencies, and no official endorsement by them should be inferred.

Originally published in *TEACHING Exceptional Children,* Vol. 39, No. 5, pp. 58–63.

9

Response to Intervention: Investigating the New Role of Special Educators

Kelli D. Cummings, Trent Atkins, Randy Allison, and Carl Cole

Special educators wear many different hats in our current educational system. Due to recent federal legislation, they may be required to wear a couple of new ones. This article provides a glimpse into past roles and begins to lay some groundwork for the future role of special educators in a Response to Intervention (RTI) context. This article (a) highlights the congruence between legislative acts impacting education, (b) explains how legislative acts can be used to help schools be more proactive in meeting the needs of struggling students, (c) describes key elements of an RTI model, (d) explains the role of formative assessment, (e) explains the application of RTI with a school-based case example, and (f) concludes with a discussion of how the current skills of special educators can support schools beginning to adopt RTI.

CONGRUENCE BETWEEN LEGISLATIVE ACTS IMPACTING EDUCATION

The Individuals With Disabilities Education Improvement Act of 2004 (IDEA, 2004) intersects with The No Child Left Behind Act of 2001 (NCLB), and these two pieces of legislation set the stage for an approach to special education eligibility and school improvement called RTI. Both IDEA 2004 and NCLB call for improving the outcomes for all students by using scientifically based instructional practices. RTI specifically requires documentation of appropriate use of scientifically based interventions before a student is referred for a traditional special education evaluation. Documentation of appropriate instructional interventions is not a new feature of eligibility determination. IDEA 1997 states that:

> In making a determination of eligibility under paragraph (4)(A), a child shall not be determined to be a child with a disability if the determinant factor for such determination is — (A) lack of appropriate instruction in reading, including the essential components of reading instruction (as is defined in section 1208(3) of the Elementary and Secondary Education Act of 1965). (20 U.S.C. 1414(b)(5)(A))

IDEA builds on the requirements of its predecessor by including specific language on the use of RTI procedures such as "a process that determines if the child responds to scientific research-based intervention as a part of the evaluation procedures" (Public Law (P.L.) 108-446 § 614 [b][6][A]; §614 [b][2 & 3]). Clearly both NCLB and IDEA give school districts the legal authority to put an RTI system in place. Implementing such a system simultaneously addresses the needs of individual students who are struggling as well as assists schools in meeting adequate yearly progress (AYP). Special education teachers, with their knowledge of assessment, instruction, and individualized interventions, are uniquely positioned to impact and assist schools as they begin to fully implement RTI procedures.

LEGISLATIVE ACTS: HELPING SPECIAL EDUCATORS BE AGENTS FOR STUDENT ACCESS TO THE CURRICULUM

Even before the implementation of the Education for All Handicapped Children Act of 1975, special education teachers differentiated instruction in order to meet the needs of individuals with disabilities. Over the course of the last few decades special educators, and the students they serve, have moved from a system in which specialized instruction was primarily provided in separate facilities to one in which students with and without disabilities are served in public school settings. However, the process of integration has always been centered on issues of access—and merely providing access to the building does not result in equity. Facilitating access to programs and curricula are the key elements of the current roles and responsibilities of today's educator. RTI, with a focus on collaboration between all school professionals and a commitment to effective strategies that support integration and student proficiency, provides an excellent opportunity for all students to have meaningful access to the general education curriculum.

To respond to the recent legislation and summarize the nearly 30 years of extensive data from both research and practice on the topic of RTI, the National Association of State Directors of Special Education (NASDSE, 2005) convened a panel of professionals to provide guidance to state and local education agencies fostering effective RTI implementation across general, remedial, and special education. Key principles outlined in the NASDSE document are that:

- School systems must reorganize to provide multiple tiers of generally effective instructional practices with a core curriculum that meets the needs of most (e.g., 80%) students.

- Across the multiple tiers, all students are provided with access to high quality instruction matching students' needs.

- Formative assessment data are gathered to document the match between students' needs and their instruction.

- RTI is evaluated across tiers using a problem-solving model of data-based decision making.

The authors of the NASDSE document note that it is not the specific roles of special education professionals that need to change, but rather the skill sets within those roles which need to broaden as schools coordinate service delivery within an RTI context. The repertoire of special educators will expand as they assist all educators with identifying student needs early, providing a differentiated core curriculum that meets students' needs, collecting formative assessment data to evaluate the effectiveness of a variety of interventions, and providing consultative services to modify support when instruction is not having the desired effect (see Figure 1 for a description of the evolution of special educators' roles).

Although the specifics of how each of the steps of the RTI process will be implemented vary from school to school, there are certain critical elements that schools must have in place. Already discussed in this article is the requirement of a continuum of generally effective instructional supports (e.g., multi-tiered approach). Following is a detailed description of the decision-making model and the assessment tools used to evaluate RTI across the continuum from general education to special education.

KEY ELEMENTS OF AN RTI MODEL

RTI is rooted in special education with the historical purpose of addressing educational needs of students. For over 20 years, researchers and practitioners have noted significant gains in both student and school-level achievement in academic and social-behavioral domains when formative evaluation, accompanied with a continuum of effective instructional techniques, were used (Heller, Holtzman, & Messick, 1982; Simmons et al., 2002). Recent councils (e.g., National Research Council, 2002; President's Council on Special Education Excellence, 2002) who have advised on the reauthorization of IDEA state that any efforts to scale up RTI ought to be based on problem-solving models which have documented effectiveness in school settings and through research (Pasternack, 2002). The challenge lies in integrating systems of

Figure 1. A Comparison and Contrast of Roles of the Special Educator in a Response to Intervention (RTI) Context

Domain	Historical Context	RTI Context
Assessment	Starting point is typically when a student is referred for special education evaluation.	Starting point is before there are serious learning problems (i.e., universal screening).
Testing Instruments	Summative (single point) assessment, typically using global achievement tests.	Formative (multiple measures using different but equivalent test forms) assessment of a student's learning over time.
Intervention	Provide intensive instruction to a relatively stable group of students within a given school year.	Provide differentiated instruction to a variety of students; grouping is flexible and dynamic.
	Service delivery is contingent upon a student's eligibility status.	Service delivery is contingent upon a student's need.
Professional Environment	Somewhat isolated. Work with general educators is relatively infrequent.	Collaborative. Consultation with educators and specialists within a building is required.

service delivery and implementing a decision-making model across the continuum of general and special education.

Outcomes Drive the Decisions

Regardless of the specific method chosen to implement RTI, research and practice have identified procedural models with key decision-making steps that promote school effectiveness and collaboration. Successful models have in common a core set of values regarding the nature of assessment. In them, assessment is linked to intervention, is formative, and is relevant to the curriculum.

Steps in an Outcomes-Driven Model

The Outcomes-Driven Model is one specific example of a useful framework for RTI implementation. This model extends previous work from problem-solving models (Deno, 1989; Shinn, 1995; Tilly, 2008) and the initial application of the problem-solving model to early literacy skills (Kaminski & Good, 1998). Yet the Outcomes-Driven Model is unique due to its focus on early intervention and universal screening. The general questions addressed by a problem-solving model include: (a) What is the problem? (b) Why is it happening? (c) What should be done about it? and (d) Did it work? (Tilly, 2008). The

Figure 2. Steps in the Outcomes-Driven Model

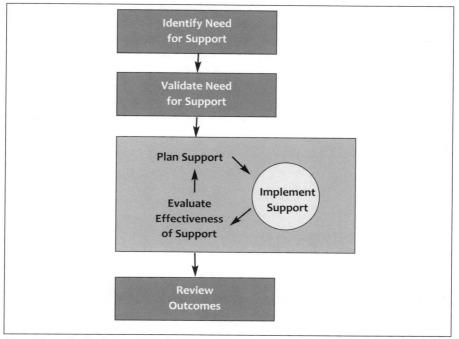

Note. "Steps in the Outcomes Driven Model," ©2007. Dynamic Measurement Group, Eugene, Oregon. Reprinted with permission.

Outcomes-Driven Model was developed to address these questions, but within a prevention-oriented framework designed to preempt early learning difficulties and ensure step-by-step progress toward important outcomes. The Outcomes-Driven Model accomplishes these goals through a set of four educational decisions: (a) identify a need for support; (b) validate the need for support; (c) plan, implement, evaluate, and modify support; and (d) review outcomes.

Identifying the Need for Support. The first step in the Outcomes-Driven Model is identifying the need for support. During this phase, universal screening occurs which consists of brief assessments administered to students in an entire school or classroom. This particular step identifies students early who might need additional instruction in order to achieve meaningful goals. Students who demonstrate low levels of performance on the screening task are red flagged for further evaluation in order to determine the level of support required to address the need. Special educators are vital members of the assessment team that collects this screening data (see Figure 2).

Validating the Need for Support. The next step is validating the need for the support identified in step one. The purpose of this step is to rule out easy reasons for a child's poor performance (i.e., child had a bad day or did not understand the directions) and to ensure that the educator is reasonably confident that the child needs additional support. One way to validate a student's need for support is to compare a student's performance on the screening assessment with other information that the teacher has about that child. If the child is new to the school or if it is the beginning of the year and no other data are readily available, the teacher may choose to assess the student across multiple days and examine the trend in performance. If the student continues to display a pattern of poor performance across at least three different assessment periods, it is presumed that the student requires additional instructional support (Kaminski, Cummings, Powell-Smith, & Good, 2008). It is important to utilize this step of the Outcomes-Driven Model so that no single piece of assessment data is used to make decisions about a student's instructional plan.

Plan, Implement, Evaluate, and Modify Support. Once the level of support is planned and details are developed for where, when, and with whom the instruction will be delivered, educators implement, evaluate, and modify that support as needed. During this phase, students' progress is monitored along their path toward a particular goal, with the frequency of the monitoring and the intensity of the intervention designed to match the students' need. For example, a student with severe needs may be monitored weekly or even twice weekly, and students with less severe needs may only need to be monitored once per month.

There are specific decision rules associated with progress monitoring used to evaluate the effectiveness of interventions. A general recommendation is the 3-point rule, where interventions are continuously evaluated and if a student's performance falls below the goal in more than 3 consecutive data points, the intervention is changed based on the specific pattern of student performance. This recommended decision rule is based on early work with curriculum-based measurement (CBM; Fuchs, 1988, 1989) and precision teaching (White & Haring, 1980). As when validating a student's need for support, a pattern of performance is considered before making individual student decisions. This iterative process continues until the student makes sufficient progress and is back on track to meet established goals. (See the "Interventions and Strategies" section of Figure 3 for references on specific intervention ideas across a variety of skill areas.)

Outcome Evaluation. Continued refinement of educational programs continues through the outcome evaluation. The premise of the Outcomes-Driven Model is that failure is not an option (Kaminski & Good, 1998). Students are monitored and intervention is evaluated until a student reaches the set goals. It is important to remember that it is not just the monitoring but the continued responsive intervention that makes the difference in a student's success.

Figure 3. Free, Electronic Resources for the Foundations of Response to Intervention (RTI)

Universal Screening and Progress Monitoring

National Center on Student Progress Monitoring
http://www.studentprogress.org/

This site provides information on the scientifically based practice of screening and monitoring students' skills. A variety of articles and descriptions of different tools are available.

Core Curricular and Supplemental Programs

Oregon Reading First Center
http://oregonreadingfirst.uoregon.edu/curriculum_review.php

This site provides a report of comprehensive core and supplemental reading programs. Programs submitted for review were analyzed and scored using a rubric developed by the Oregon Reading First Center.

Interventions and Strategies

Florida Center on Reading Research
http://www.fcrr.org/Interventions/index.htm

This site provides multiple intervention ideas linked to the five big ideas of early reading. Interventions for individuals or small groups can be printed in their entirety.

Intervention Central

http://www.interventioncentral.org/

This site provides interventions and strategies for reading and other skills areas. The site allows educational professionals to develop individual assessment instruments.

THE ROLE OF FORMATIVE ASSESSMENT

The systematic and recursive feedback loops (i.e., teach, assess, and modify teaching as needed) of the Outcomes-Driven Model, and more globally the RTI process, require a new perspective on assessment practices where the key decision is not one of high-stakes eligibility or evaluation but one of instructional planning. Formative assessment is the process by which data are used to adapt teaching to students' needs (Kaminski & Cummings, 2007).

One type of formative assessment tool is general outcome measures (GOMs). GOMs differ from other types of formative assessments in that they are standardized, establish psychometric properties, and provide different but equivalent alternate forms for progress monitoring. These key features are necessary to consider when determining appropriate assessments within an RTI model. These features of GOMs facilitate the necessary comparisons between students, as in the case of universal screening. Also, GOMs are ideally suited to repeated measurement over time, thus providing a means to engage in progress monitoring of individual students.

CBM is one widely known type of GOM that allows educators to quickly and efficiently assess students' growth in basic skill areas (Shinn, 2002). More recently, data have converged to suggest that GOMs can be used to broadly support a wider range of educational decisions including screening in general education and linking performance on these brief measures to high-stakes tests as required for NCLB. GOMs are widely available for assessing early reading skills (Good & Kaminski, 2002) as well as infant and pre-schooler development (Carta et al., 2002). See Figure 3 for more information regarding formative assessment technologies.

The aforementioned assessment tools are a means by which educators can determine that (a) students have an appropriate intervention with which to respond and (b) that the response is sufficient to result in meaningful changes in outcomes for a student. A common feature to each GOM is that they are indicators of broader skill areas. GOMs do not assess everything about a particular domain, but they assess important things about that domain. Students' patterns of performance on these measures directly relate to performance on important developmental tasks. For instance, one of the most widely used and researched GOMs, Oral Reading Fluency, is a very powerful indicator of the global domain of overall reading skill and comprehension.

GOMs are also dynamic in that they are sensitive to small but meaningful gains in student improvement over time. Because GOMs are designed to be brief, educators can use them weekly if needed in order to determine if the intervention is working or if the interventions need to be modified. If interventions need to be changed, an educator has additional insight about what specific skills to teach based on the student's performance during these brief assessments. This aspect of GOMs represents the feature of being authentic assessments, wherein the skills that are assessed match the instruction that is delivered, and that instruction is continually evaluated. Student outcomes drive the decisions in this process.

APPLICATION OF THE RTI MODEL

Changing the focus of assessment and the nature of intervention plays a critical yet varied role in effective RTI implementation. In an RTI model, it is presupposed that referrals for higher levels of intervention are based on data. As a result, referrals for special education are likely to include information that is more relevant for eligibility decision making and instructional planning than in the past. Because all children are screened for early skill deficits, children are able to access curriculum in the least restrictive environment. As general education teachers begin to teach to a wider variety of students, special educators take on an expanded role in providing consultative assistance to their general education colleagues.

The Outcomes-Driven Model addresses prevention needs across the continuum. The intention of the Outcomes-Driven Model is that a student's needs are addressed before referrals to special education for learning disabilities are needed. This requires a component of systems-level evaluation which increases accountability and ultimately helps plan instructional support for all students. Research continues to demonstrate that progress monitoring (e.g., formative assessment) substantially increases the effectiveness of intervention. Studies further document that the effectiveness of progress monitoring increases when graphing techniques and decision rules are used (Fuchs & Fuchs, 1986; Kavale, 2005). The practice of progress monitoring may take place in both general education and special education; its frequency and intensity is what will change depending upon student need.

Important changes in special education result from the general education application of collecting formative assessment data within an Outcomes-Driven Model. By linking assessment with interventions, educators document what is special about special education. The decisions accompanying each of these steps in the Outcomes-Driven Model are congruent with the argument made by Ysseldyke and Marston (1998) that our eligibility decisions ought to be based on instructional efforts to help all students achieve better outcomes. Special education is therefore not a place; rather, it is a set of interventions designed to ensure individual student success.

When problem solving across the continuum is generalized, it is found that the purpose of RTI is not a cheaper, faster way of identifying students for special education. Rather, it is a way of ensuring that students are provided with what they need to succeed in education. Special educators play a critical role in evaluating the effectiveness of a variety of interventions within their classrooms and schools.

A Case Study

To illustrate how the role of the special educator might change in an RTI model, review the case study in Figure 4 describing one school district's path toward RTI implementation. This description, provided by an administrator, details how RTI was initiated nearly 5 years prior to the time of this publication. In this example, the district was able to maximize student learning and reduce the rates of referral to special education.

Possible New Roles for Special Educators

As RTI processes are considered and tested across increasing numbers of school systems, the role of teachers in this process needs to be a significant consideration, especially for special education teachers. The success of core instruction with all students in general education becomes a critical determination. It is most likely the success or failure of this differentiated core

Figure 4. Case Study: One District's Experience With Response to Intervention (RTI) Scale Up and Implementation

Tell us a little bit about your school. Our school district is located in a suburban town in the northwest part of the United States. This particular area is experiencing rapid growth with a number of transient hotels and subsidized low-income housing. Associated with the economics of the community, 45% of the students qualify for free/reduced lunch and there is a high mobility and student turnover rate. The district historically has had a large number of students receiving special education services, averaging 15% of the total population. The district has a high quality, special education staff with training in both current assessment practices and research-based instructional programs.

How did you begin to scale up RTI? The school district began moving several years ago to an RTI model as an outgrowth of a districtwide reading project utilizing research-based reading programs. The project was initiated in response to the large number of students needing special education services to address reading deficiencies. Prior to implementing the research-based reading project, a large number of students here were referred and identified for special education who lacked exposure to effective instruction within the general education curriculum. Within this approach, special education teachers participated in the identification of students who could best be described as instructionally disabled, believing that only within the special education curriculum would they have access to programs appropriate to students' needs. We thus began to scale up RTI by bringing special education resources, including special education teachers, to bear within our overall instructional environment.

What were the goals of the new program? The goal of the program was to involve both general and special education teachers who work on school reading teams to select and implement high quality research-based assessments and reading programs. General and special education teachers worked as a team to select primary, secondary, and tertiary reading programs, and instruction was delivered on a continuum rather than categorically. By utilizing special education teachers to help differentiate the core curriculum, we were able to serve our students more effectively and efficiently. The district also adopted the Dynamic Indicators of Basic Early Literacy Skills (DIBELS) and Test of Oral Reading Fluency (TORF) as formative assessment tools to identify early reading discrepancies through universal screening and to monitor student progress.

What are some of the key outcomes of this project? Through the early identification of struggling readers within the general education population, it was possible to deliver targeted instruction within general education, Title I services, or special education. Reading teams, composed of special and general education teachers, were reluctant to refer students to special education without exploring every available research-based intervention and closely monitoring the student's progress. This process of evaluating how students responded to interventions led the teams to no longer focus on the student's perceived discrepancy but to make sure that the student had every opportunity to learn. The reading project had many outcomes both intended and unintended.

How did these changes support an RTI Framework? The project resulted in a restructuring of the instructional program and the elimination of categorical barriers between special and general education. The stated goal of the project was to provide quality, research-based instruction and reduce the incidence for reading disabilities, which was achieved in a dramatic fashion. With the implementation of effective practices in reading, the elementary school referral rates fell to single-digit percentages districtwide! The unintended result was the district evolving to an RTI model as a result of practice rather than policy shift—most significantly the instructional melding between general and special education. Students in our district now have the benefit of a wide array of instructional opportunities among general education, Title I services, and special education without having to cross categorical barriers.

instruction that leads to potential referral for additional services, which in many cases includes special education. How special education teachers position themselves to support and supplement core instruction or align themselves to provide intensive intervention is critical to the RTI process in general, and specifically to the special education teachers' value in the system. (See Figure 5 for a description of key roles of the special education teacher in an RTI model.) The bottom line is that no matter how student problems are identified, unless educators provide meaningful and effective instruction, student progress will not change.

Special education teachers should be able to help support RTI efforts across varied problem areas and various programming options. To be assistive to the RTI model, special education teachers need to support efforts to implement a problem-solving framework premised on four basic questions:

- What is the student's problem and why is it happening?
- What is the best instructional plan for the student given the analysis of the concern?
- How can the plan be implemented as it was conceived and data collected for analysis of performance?
- Are the desired results being achieved as expected or do changes need to be made?

A further analysis of these foundational concepts helps clarify a special education teacher's increasing role in creating a successful learning experience for all children.

An important role of the special education teacher is helping others understand how to evaluate a target student's concern in comparison to an accepted standard of success. This gap analysis is fundamental in an RTI model and sets the stage for an analysis of the problem that is subsequently defined. Looking for probable causes of the learning problems defined in this way is a critical step in the process. It allows special education teachers to help other educators look more deeply at why a student may have problems in specific areas and potentially successful interventions. Helping define, validate, and analyze problems at an individual and group level is a critical skill for special education teachers in a successful RTI model.

Special education teachers are often seen as a wealth of information on instructional strategies that are effective with students with disabilities. Therefore, once a student's problems are defined and accurately analyzed, special educators help other educators with consideration of scientifically based and researched instructional strategies to be used. By linking reliable instructional strategies which match the analyzed need of a student, the likelihood of intervention success is greatly increased. Special education teachers help establish meaningful goals for student attainment and meaningful methods of monitoring progress towards those goals.

After a well conceived plan is developed, the special education teacher provides modeling, support, and feedback on the implementation of the inter-

Figure 5. List of Key Activities for Special Educators in a Response to Intervention (RTI) Model Linked to the Outcomes-Driven Model

Key Activity	Step in the Outcomes-Driven Model
1. Evaluate a target student's concern in comparison to an accepted standard of success. Assist and/or train the school's universal screening team to administer formative assessments (e.g., Dynamic Indicators of Basic Early Literacy Skills and other curriculum-based measurements) with fidelity.	**Identify Need for Support**
2. Assist in the consideration of scientifically based instructional strategies. Use knowledge of student skill and error patterns for more advanced educational diagnosis.[a]	**Plan & Implement Support**
3. Provide modeling, support, and feedback to other professionals regarding intervention implementation. Use understanding of reading student graphs to assist others in interpreting a student's rate of progress.	**Evaluate & Modify Support**
4. Participate in ongoing formative assessment and summative evaluation of intervention effectiveness. Consult with general education teachers and other professionals to enhance teaching activities.	**Outcomes Evaluation**

[a]We use the term *educational diagnosis* here in a manner similar to Howell & Nolet (2000), by stating that it ought to be a teaching decision rather than an entitlement decision. An educational diagnosis according to this paradigm thus includes two key elements: effectively identifying what to teach and how to teach it.

vention. Some special education teachers may even find themselves collaboratively working with general education teachers with intervention groups or teaching intervention groups of like-need students. The knowledge of what and how to teach hard-to-reach students is an important role of special education teachers.

Finally, special education teachers become involved in ongoing, formative assessments as well as summative evaluation. By virtue of their work with individualized education programs, special educators help teachers less familiar with data collection, data analysis, and decision-making procedures. Assisting less familiar teachers with these tasks uses special education teachers' expertise on instructional and curricular needs for students who are not making adequate progress or need additional instructional considerations to enhance the level of progress made. The idea of formatively monitoring the effects of instruction and analyzing student performance results to make instructional changes is a strength of many special education teachers.

Too often, concerns are expressed that the need for special education teachers will be reduced through effective intervention practices. Looking holistically at the needs within a systemic response to intervention approach, that concern does not seem well grounded given the knowledge, skills, and resources that special education teachers offer the overall system.

CONCLUSION

The RTI process is about more than special education eligibility; it is ultimately a focus on school improvement to build effective systems of service delivery. The special education teacher is in a unique position to contribute to the way in which such a service delivery model plays out within a school. Throughout the process of collaboration, the special education teacher is viewed as a key consultant assisting with planning, implementation, and evaluation of interventions across the continuum of education. Special education teachers also experience increased involvement with general education and Title I staff by way of early screening activities, collaborative instructional processes for groups of students with similar skills, and interpreting RTI data within the context of the problem-solving process. The special educator in an RTI model plays a key role in enhancing instructional opportunity for all students.

The skills that special education teachers bring to the table may ultimately result in fewer students qualifying for specialized services. However, rather than seeing this outcome as working oneself out of a job, it should be viewed as an opportunity to focus more intensely on the students with the most severe needs and help provide more effective instruction for all students.

REFERENCES

Carta, J. J., Greenwood, C. R., Walker, D., Kaminski, R., Good, R., McConnell, S., & McEvoy, M. (2002). Individual growth and development indicators (IGDIs): Assessment that guides intervention for young children. In M. Ostrosky & E. Horn (Eds.). *Assessment: Gathering meaningful information.* The Young Exceptional Children Monograph Series #4. Longmont, CO: Sopris West. Retrieved January 8, 2008, from http://www.igdi.ku.edu/documents/ index.htm

Deno, S. L. (1989). Curriculum-based measurement and special education services: A fundamental and direct relationship. In M. R. Shinn (Ed.), *Curriculum-based measurement: Assessing special children* (pp. 1–17). New York: Guilford.

Dynamic Measurement Group. (2007). "Steps in the outcomes-driven model." Eugene, OR: Author.

Fuchs, L. S. (1988). Effects of computer-managed instruction on teachers' implementation of systematic monitoring programs, student achievement, and student awareness of learning. *Journal of Educational Research, 81,* 294–304.

Fuchs, L. S. (1989). Evaluating solutions: Monitoring progress and revising intervention plans. In M. Shinn (Ed.), *Curriculum-based measurement: Assessing special children* (pp. 153–181). New York: Guilford.

Fuchs, L. S., & Fuchs, D. (1986). Effects of systematic formative evaluation: A meta-analysis. *Exceptional Children, 53,* 199–208.

Good, R. H., & Kaminski, R. A. (Eds.). (2002). *Dynamic indicators of basic early literacy skills* (6th ed.). Eugene, OR: Institute for the Development of Educational Achievement. Retrieved January 8, 2008, from http://dibels.uoregon.edu/

Heller, K. A., Holtzman, W., & Messick, S. (1982). Placement in special education: Historical developments and current procedures. In K. A. Heller, W. H. Holtzman, & S. Messick (Eds.), *Placing children in special education: A strategy for equity* (pp. 23–44). Washington, DC: National Academy Press.

Howell, K. W. & Nolet, V. (2000). *Curriculum-based evaluation: teaching and decision making* (3rd ed.). Canada: Wadsworth.

Individuals With Disabilities Act of 1997. Reauthorization of P.L. 105-17.

Individuals With Disabilities Education Improvement Act of 2004, P. L. 108-466.

Kaminski, R. A., & Cummings, K. D. (2007, Winter). Assessment for learning: Using general outcomes measures. *Threshold,* 26–28.

Kaminski, R. A., Cummings, K. D., Powell-Smith, K. A., & Good, R. H. (2008). Best practices in using dynamic indicators of basic early literacy skills (DIBELS®) for formative assessment and evaluation. In A. Thomas & J. Grimes (Eds.). *Best practices in school psychology V* (pp. 1181–1204). Bethesda, MD: National Association of School Psychologists.

Kaminski, R. A., & Good, R. H. (1998). Assessing early literacy skills in a problem-solving model: Dynamic indicators of basic early literacy skills. In M. R. Shinn (Ed.), *Advanced applications of CBM* (pp. 113–142). New York: Guilford.

Kavale, K. (2005). Effective intervention for students with specific learning disability: The nature of special education. *Learning Disabilities, 13*(4), 127–138.

National Association of State Directors of Special Education. (2005). *Response to Intervention: Policy considerations and implementation.* Alexandria, VA: Author.

National Research Council. (2002). *Executive summary. Disproportionate representation of minority students in special education.* Washington, DC: Author.

No Child Left Behind Act of 2001, P. L. 107-110.

Pasternack, R. H. (2002, March). *The demise of IQ testing for children with learning disabilities.* Paper presented at the meeting of the National Association of School Psychologists 2002 Annual Convention, Chicago, IL.

President's Council on Special Education Excellence. (2002). *A NEW ERA: Revitalizing special education for children and their families.* Washington, DC: U.S. Department of Education.

Shinn, M. R. (1995). Best practices in curriculum-based measurement and its use in a problem-solving model. In A. Thomas & J. Grimes (Eds.), *Best practices in school psychology III* (pp. 547–567). Washington, DC: National Association of School Psychologists.

Shinn, M. R. (2002). Best Practices in using curriculum based measurement in a problem-solving model. In A. Thomas & J. Grimes (Eds.). *Best practices in school psychology IV* (pp. 671–697). Bethesda, MD: National Association of School Psychologists. Retrieved January 8, 2008, from http://www.nasponline.org/trainers/BPIV/44-Shinn.pdf

Simmons, D. C., Kame'enui, E. J., Good, R. H., Harn, B. A., Cole, C., & Braun, D. (2002). Building, implementing, and sustaining a beginning reading improvement model: Lessons learned school by school. In M. R. Shinn, H. M. Walker, & G.

Stoner (Eds.). *Interventions for academic and behavior problems II: Preventive and remedial approaches* (pp. 537–570). Bethesda, MD: National Association of School Psychologists.

Tilly, W. D. (2008). The evolution of school psychology to science-based practice. In A. Thomas & J. Grimes (Eds.). *Best practices in school psychology V* (pp. 17–36). Bethesda, MD: National Association of School Psychologists.

White, O. R., & Haring, N. G. (1980). *Exceptional teaching* (2nd ed.). Columbus, OH: Merrill.

Ysseldyke, J., & Marston, D. (1998). Origins of categorical special education services in schools and a rationale for changing them. In D. J. Reschly, W. D. Tilly III, & J. P. Grimes (Eds.). *Special education in transition: Functional assessment and noncategorical programming* (pp. 1–18). Longmont, CO: Sopris West.

This manuscript was supported by the Schools and Communities Coming Together Project at the Division of Educational Research and Service, The University of Montana and Federal Grants 2003CKWX0274 and 2004CKWX0377 from the Community Oriented Policing Services Office, U.S. Department of Justice. However, no official university or federal endorsement should be inferred.

Originally published in *TEACHING Exceptional Children*, Vol. 40, No. 4, pp. 24–31.

10

Implementation of Response to Intervention at Middle School: Challenges and Potential Benefits

Evelyn Sue Johnson and Lori Smith

Middle school represents a major transition in a student's academic career. For most students, it means changing schools, adjusting to a longer school day, changing teachers for content courses, and meeting demands of more complex assignments requiring independent learning and critical thinking skills. Given these challenges, the fact that many students require additional support to experience academic success in middle school is not surprising. For a variety of reasons, such as existing learning difficulties, increased academic demands, language proficiency, and transience, early interventions to support success in middle school are routinely needed for an increasingly large and diverse population of students.

Well-documented, research-based interventions are available for middle school students, but one problem that limits their effective implementation is the lack of a schoolwide process through which to do so. The result is a haphazard approach to intervention, with no coordination across classrooms and limited information on efficacy. Providing interventions in an effective manner—one that responds to individual student needs and supports progress in the general curriculum—poses significant challenges at the middle school level.

A MIDDLE SCHOOL RESPONSE-TO-INTERVENTION MODEL

One model that can help middle school educators provide an effective system of instruction and early intervention is response to intervention (RTI). RTI is

Figure 1. Academic and Behavioral Tiered-Service-Delivery Model in Use at Cheyenne Mountain Junior High School

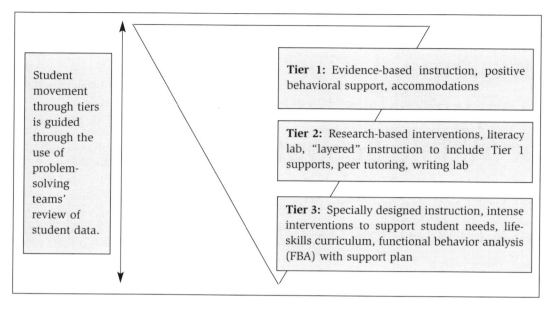

a schoolwide process that integrates instruction, intervention, and assessment. The alignment of instruction, assessment, and interventions promotes a stronger, more cohesive program of instruction that ultimately can result in higher student achievement (Mellard & Johnson, 2008).

The recent focus in the literature and related policy initiatives on RTI presents a welcome opportunity to structure a more comprehensive and integrated approach to instruction and intervention for all students. RTI is proposed as a valuable model for educators because of its potential utility in the provision of appropriate learning experiences for all students as well as in the early identification of students as being at risk for academic failure. As described in the literature (Fuchs & Fuchs, 2006; Johnson, Mellard, Fuchs, & McKnight, 2006), a strong RTI process includes the following crucial features:

- High-quality, scientifically based classroom instruction.
- Schoolwide screening of academics and behavior.
- Progress monitoring of student performance.
- Implementation of research-based interventions at all tiers.
- Fidelity checks on implementation.

RTI models continue to be researched and implemented in elementary school settings. Although state agencies and practitioners conceptually embrace the RTI concept for older students as well, scant research and few, if any, RTI models appropriate for secondary school settings exist. The need for successful models of RTI implementation at the middle school level is great, because middle school represents a crucial point in a student's academic career, laying the foundation for successful completion of high school (Morris, Ehren & Lenz, 1991). Middle and high school students deal with a demanding curriculum no longer focused on the acquisition of basic skills; rather they must rely on those basic skills for acquiring content knowledge (Deshler, Hock & Catts, 2006; Deshler & Schumaker, 2006; Swanson, 2001). Intervention models can support students who struggle with these demands.

One challenge for successful implementation of RTI at the middle school level is that much of the literature on the RTI process tends to support the use of standard protocol approaches (Fuchs, Mock, Morgan, & Young, 2003); that is, evidenced-based, standard interventions with specified materials and procedures. But many standard intervention protocols are geared toward the early grades, with few secondary-level interventions having the same level of scientific base on which to support their use. Alternative approaches to intervention in an RTI framework include a problem-solving model (Kovaleski, 2003), in which school teams collect and analyze individual student data, and then develop plans for related interventions based on the individual student needs (Fuchs et al.). Although this approach is familiar to many educators in that it mirrors current student-study teams, evidence is lacking that such approaches lead to improved student outcomes (Fuchs et al.). This gap between the emerging research and classroom practice requires middle schools to draw on existing information across several bodies of literature to develop an RTI model that conforms with the general characteristics of effective RTI and with the specific challenges of the school. In this article, we describe one middle school's approach to developing an RTI model, using the existing literature as a framework for presenting the implementation process and evaluating areas in which improvement and continued attention will be needed for success.

STARTING THE PROCESS OF RTI IMPLEMENTATION

Cheyenne Mountain Junior High School teachers began implementation of the RTI process during the 2006 to 2007 school year. The school population is 84% Caucasian, 8% Hispanic, 5% Asian, and 2% African American. Ten percent of the students are English language learners, 5% of the students receive special education services, and 8% qualify for free or reduced-price lunch programs. Twenty percent of the population comes from "out of district," and a growing number of students are being retained in seventh and eighth grades. The increase in the "out of district" population has been a result of declining enrollments within the immediate community and has increased the diversity of both the ethnic and socioeconomic demographics of the school. As the school population continues to change, Cheyenne Mountain educators realized their need for a schoolwide process to improve the instructional and intervention system for their students.

The school's existing approach to schoolwide behavioral support, modeled on the Positive Behavior Support model (Sugai, Horner, & Gresham, 2002), provided a strong foundation for the decision to use a problem-solving approach. The proactive stance of positive behavior support helped the educators make the needed paradigm shift to a tiered model of service delivery. Because the school already relied on problem-solving teams for individual students in need of more intense behavior supports, that approach was expanded to include meeting the academic needs of the students. After reviewing the existing literature on RTI, the first decision the educators made was to expand the current problem-solving approach for planning and implementing interventions. The problem-solving approach to RTI was chosen over the standard-protocol approach because of the current lack of standard protocols for middle school students. However, an all-school goal is to create a bank of interventions to address individual students' academic needs, as well as to support success in the general curriculum. In effect, the problem-solving approach was chosen initially, with a goal of expanding the use of standard protocols that the teachers could later draw on to match an intervention with an individual student's specific needs.

An overview of the school's tiered-service-delivery model is depicted in Figure 1. As is shown, a proactive approach to both behavior and academics is applied through the focus on positive behavior support, schoolwide discipline, and the use of differentiated instruction. Students are screened for academic and behavioral concerns, and this assessment information is compiled for the school's problem-solving team (PST) to review. The school expanded its existing problem-solving-team approach for behavioral concerns to also address academic concerns. The PST then recommends appropriate interventions and supports for the student of concern; the student's progress with these supports is monitored; and decisions to continue, modify or withdraw the intervention are made accordingly. Each of these steps is explained in more detail below.

TIER 1: INSTRUCTION IN THE GENERAL CLASSROOM

One of the main advantages of an RTI model is its emphasis on ensuring appropriate learning opportunities for all students, beginning in the general education classroom. The system of screening and progress monitoring, contained within an iterative process of data collection, analysis, and decision making, supports a proactive approach to ensuring academic success (Mellard & Johnson, 2008). Therefore, one of the first areas reviewed was the general education instruction provided to students. Under tiered models of service delivery, 80% to 85% of the general population should be successful at the first tier of intervention (Vaughn, 2003), with no need of further intervention if the instruction is effective.

To determine the effectiveness of instruction at Cheyenne Mountain, schoolwide state testing scores were reviewed in reading, mathematics, science, and writing, indicating that at least 80% of the students were meeting standards (Colorado Student Assessment Program, *Summary Report, 2005–2006*, pp. 1–7). However, observations of practice as well as dialogue in departmental professional learning communities (DuFour & Eaker, 1998) found that the use of differentiation in instruction was one practice that could be improved, especially given the concerns of an increasingly diverse population of students. Additionally, the junior high school had more than 120 identified highly capable students who were not receiving any enrichment or enhancement in their homework, assessments, or direct instruction. Also, no supports were employed for students with learning difficulties within the general classroom, even though the school follows an inclusion model for serving students in special education. A school-level goal for improving the general education instruction was to provide professional development in differentiation and to establish timelines for implementation through the use of departmental professional learning communities.

At the end of the first year of implementation, the importance of differentiating instruction within each classroom has been realized. By focusing professional development on ways to differentiate, teachers have developed a greater knowledge of and ability to apply such strategies. For example, the English department has begun to provide a range of options for book reports to include essays, scrapbooks, newspapers, or video production so that students can demonstrate their understanding of literary elements without relying completely on writing skills. Student completion of these projects increased substantially as a result of being offered such choices. Within the social studies department, teachers have begun using unit preassessments based on unit essential questions. Through this process, they are able to determine appropriate placement of students within a range of activities, interests, and goals for the specific lesson. Assessment continues throughout the lesson to modify instruction and allow for flexible grouping. This formative assessment is based on numerous observations, including the use of clickers by students to indicate when they have not comprehended material. The most beneficial aspect of the increased focus on differentiation has been the teachers' heightened awareness that different types of learners are present within each classroom and that instruction can be designed in numerous ways to meet their needs.

Universal Screening

At the time of developing the RTI model, Cheyenne Mountain Junior High had no system for universal screening in the essential academic areas. Instead, students with potential learning problems were identified through teacher referrals, parental concerns, or performance on state tests, none of which supported efforts for early intervention. As a school, the goal of implementing curriculum-based assessments in reading, writing, and mathematics, and establishing a process by which data on student performance could be collected, reviewed, and analyzed several times during the academic year, was set. A screening schedule of fall, winter, and spring allowed for targeting students in the beginning of the school year to provide interventions early, as well as for monitoring students who were initially successful but then became overwhelmed by shifting demands later in the school year. The spring assessments provide information on students who might require intervention through summer intervention programs, as well as targets students for early intervention in the subsequent academic year.

In reading, the school used the diagnostic assessment of reading (DAR) to screen for students at risk. Performance on this assessment is provided in grade-level equivalents. Students who perform at the fifth-grade equivalent or below are referred for targeted intervention (explained in the next section). Procedures and decision rules for targeting students who are below grade-level equivalent but not significantly below (e.g., an eighth grader reading at a sixth-grade equivalent) are being developed. For mathematics, Cheyenne Mountain Junior High is using the Performance Series assessments (Scantron, 2007) to provide information on student abilities on various mathematics skills. The school is working on developing decision rules for targeting students for intervention. The information received from the Performance Series assessment will provide one source of data to guide those decisions. Students at risk for writing problems are identified using state test scores from the previous year and an introductory paragraph assessment conducted by English teachers.

The screening data are then compiled on a student data sheet (see Figure 2) that also includes teacher narratives and comments about the student's academic performance and behavior. Student performance and data are collected on these sheets and submitted to the PST for review at monthly meetings. The implementation of effective screening tools remains an area of continued review for the school. Identification rates for intervention and the subsequent outcomes will continue to guide the refinement of screening instruments.

TIER 2: INTERVENTIONS

In an RTI framework, interventions for students who are not successful in the general classroom are provided at Tier 2. This level is designed for students who do not achieve to grade-level standards when provided with generally effective Tier 1 instruction. Interventions in Tier 2 are intended to be targeted to a specific academic skill, provided for a limited duration (between 8 and 12 weeks), and delivered in small groups, with regular progress monitoring to determine the effect of the intervention (Vaughn, 2003).

At Cheyenne Mountain, the existing resources to provide interventions are limited. Therefore, in initial stages of RTI implementation, reading was the primary focus given its impact across the curriculum. Additionally, on the basis of research on layered interventions (McMaster, Fuchs, Fuchs, & Compton, 2005), the school adopted a model of intervention that included

Figure 2. Cheyenne Mountain Junior High Student Data Summary

Cheyenne Mountain Junior High Student Data Summary

This summary sheet is used to gather and review student data before the problem-solving-team meeting.

Student Name: **Date:**

Grade: **Age:**   **Primary Home Language:** *English*

Parents/Guardians: **Address:**   **Phone:**

Siblings:

HEALTH INFORMATION

Vision Assessment: Hearing Assessment:

Significant Medical History:

Physical Health Concerns:

# of visits to Nurse: Comments:

School History

Comments:

Friends:

ACADEMIC ASSESSMENTS

	CSAP: 6th		ITBS: Yr/Sc.		ITBS: Yr/Sc.
Reading					
SS					
Mathematics					
Other					

COGAT:

DISCIPLINE HISTORY

	None	Dates	Describe Incidents
Expulsions			
Suspensions			
Office Referrals			
Other			

OUTSIDE AGENCIES

Are any other agencies/practitioners providing services for the student/family?

STUDENT INPUT

What I do best in school:

How I get along with classmates/peers:

How I get along with teachers:

Areas I could use the most improvement:

Things that are most difficult for me at school:

The one thing I'd like to focus on to make me more successful:

What helps me learn best:

Other:

PARENT INPUT

Student's academic strengths:

Student's academic concerns:

Student's social/emotional/behavioral strengths:

Student's social/emotional/behavioral concerns:

Successful academic interventions used:

Successful social/emotional/behavioral interventions used:

Other relevant information:

TEACHER INPUT

Student's academic strengths:

Student's academic concerns:

Student's social/emotional/behavioral strengths:

Student's social/emotional/behavioral concerns:

Successful academic interventions:

Successful social/emotional interventions:

Other relevant information/Grades:

Suggested Assessments:

Suggested Classroom Interventions:

Other Pertinent Information:

Progress Monitoring:

enhanced instruction (through differentiation and the use of accommodations) and schoolwide instruction on study skills within the general education classroom, combined with targeted small-group intervention for students at risk. Thus, a student in Tier 2 could receive accommodations and differentiated instruction combined with schoolwide interventions within the general education setting.

For example, to support students with difficulties in reading, the school has a "literacy lab" elective. All students at Cheyenne Mountain have two elective courses, during which they might take music, art, or a foreign language. Students identified for interventions and their parents are asked to use one of those elective times to enroll in the literacy lab. Under the supervision of the school's reading specialist, the literacy lab uses the Language! (Greene, 1999) program and other supported reading opportunities to increase students' reading achievement. These students also receive such accommodations as advanced organizers in the general education class to support their reading comprehension as they continue to increase their reading ability.

Resources to support writing and mathematics were more restricted at Cheyenne Mountain and remain limited. Goals for developing writing and mathematics labs to support the needs of students at risk for underachievement have been established. Interventions in mathematics and writing will follow the layered approach adopted in reading, in which students receive support in a small-group intervention, as well as accompanying support to ensure their successful progress in the general classroom.

Overall, the school has worked at creating several Tier 2 interventions for recurring needs. One of the most effective interventions developed at Cheyenne Mountain has been an after-school tutoring program in reading. Approximately 50% of the students enrolled in this program have made significant gains in their reading comprehension and have improved their grades substantially. On the basis of the success of this program, the RTI team recommended developing an "access" period at the end of the school day, during which students could access their teachers or other students to receive help on assignments, projects, and science labs. Without the staff's review of student progress in the tutoring intervention and subsequent dialogue, the development of this intervention would not have been possible.

Progress Monitoring

To determine whether students are benefiting from instruction and interventions, teachers must routinely collect and analyze evidence of performance. The data collected help teachers make informed subsequent instructional decisions at both the classroom and individual levels (Fuchs & Fuchs, 2006). For example, if many children in a classroom are not performing to benchmark standards, this outcome may indicate that the curriculum or instruction should be reviewed. If an individual student is not performing to standard, careful monitoring of that student's progress can help teachers devise effective interventions to support his or her learning. Frequent assessments of the relevant skills provide data on which to base decisions, such as changing the instructional program or referring a student to another tier of intervention. This systematic process, known as progress monitoring, lies at the heart of the RTI model (Mellard & Johnson, 2008).

An essential feature absent from Cheyenne Mountain Junior High's existing intervention process was the use of routine progress monitoring and data-based decision making. One final goal of the school is to identify appropriate measurements of student progress to determine whether an intervention has been effective for a particular student. As interventions with established efficacy data are identified, the school can adopt procedures described in the literature to measure their effectiveness and to implement interventions with existing assessment tools. In the interim, teacher-developed assessments of student performance along with student work samples will be evaluated more routinely to determine student progress and guide decision making. Progress monitoring remains a focus for professional development at the school.

TIER 3: INTERVENTIONS

In a three-tiered model of intervention, Tier 3 is generally synonymous with special education. One potential benefit of an RTI framework is that through early identification and intervention, the number of students requiring Tier 3 interventions will be reduced. A significant challenge of designing Tier 3 interventions, however, is selecting interventions that go beyond those implemented at Tier 2 so as to truly address the individual needs of students.

Tier 3 proved to be the most challenging to implement at Cheyenne Mountain Junior High School because its current service delivery model is based primarily on inclusion. To demonstrate one example of how Tier 3 is currently implemented at Cheyenne Mountain, we provide the following description. The implementation team identified a small number of students who failed to make progress after three months of intervention in Tiers 1 and 2. The parents of a student who failed to make progress despite being provided accommodations and being assigned to the literacy lab were asked to attend a meeting to discuss the student's progress, and the student was assigned to a study-skills course led by the special education teacher. By the end of 6 weeks, another meeting to review the student's progress was held, and together with the parents, the team concurred that the student was still not making adequate progress as demonstrated by student work and assessment data. Because this student also had behavioral concerns that seemed to interfere with his ability to achieve academically, the team decided to integrate behavior modification therapy in conjunction with the academic interventions to support this student. This meeting occurred near the end of the school year, and the student will begin the next school year with the combination of interventions. Without the RTI framework, this student may have languished the entire year in the general education class or a study skills class that was not effective in meeting his specific needs.

Other examples of current approaches to Tier 3 at Cheyenne Mountain include the provision of a life-skills curriculum offered for students with moderate to severe disabilities. Although these students are included within the general education program for a majority of the day, these students require a curriculum that fosters the skills needed to perform such activities as self-care, community access, and work skills. In this regard, Tier 3 is designed to provide individualized instruction to meet the needs of students with more severe cognitive limitations.

CONCLUSIONS

At the end of the first year of implementation of RTI, Cheyenne Mountain has realized significant improvements in many areas. First, the systematic process of collecting evidence and evaluating performance at all levels of instruction has been invaluable in focusing efforts on improved instruction and interventions for students. Without the implementation of RTI and the focus on developing a professional learning community, the school would not have seen the concerted effort on implementing such instructional practices as differentiation across the entire school. At best, one or two teachers may have attempted its implementation. In addition, the review and analysis of interventions to target common academic concerns allows the school to use resources more efficiently and see greater student progress and a reduction in the referrals to special education services. Second, the implementation of screening and progress-monitoring tools, although still in its infancy, provides an objective means of early identification of student needs. Early identification is important given the shift in student demographics and the need to maintain an objective and nondiscriminatory system of screening for academic and behavior problems (Donovan & Cross, 2002). Finally, the information that is collected on individual students, which includes a consistent description of the instruction and interventions attempted along with the student's response to such intervention, provided the implementation team with a more substantial and organized method of communicating concerns with parents and working in conjunction with them to address student concerns.

Along with these benefits, the Cheyenne Mountain team has identified several challenges that will focus efforts in subsequent years of implementation. For example, as schools consider implementation of RTI, a primary concern will be the cost of implementation to individual schools that must meet the increasing demands of numerous underfunded policy initiatives, an increasingly diverse student population, and increasing high stakes attached to performance on state assessments. Cheyenne Mountain Junior High began the process of implementation without any additional funding allocation. However, after the first year, a reallocation of funding will be necessary to support professional development to enhance Tier 1 and Tier 2 instruction and interventions, as well as related screening and progress-monitoring tools.

The Cheyenne Mountain team has outlined the following areas as priorities as the school continues to improve its RTI approach:

- Develop a standard protocol "bank" of interventions for both academic and behavioral concerns.

- Identify and educate staff on methods of differentiating instruction, with a stronger focus on curriculum-based measurement (CBM) and on pre-assessment and postassessment strategies to monitor student progress.

- Improve communication with parents of students requiring interventions.

- Review and adopt progress-monitoring tools, such as CBMs and recording protocols, to monitor student data and movement throughout the tiers.

Implementation of RTI, particularly at the middle school level, where specific recommendations are currently lacking, will be an ongoing process of identifying appropriate instructional approaches and related interventions, providing professional development to staff charged with implementation, and ensuring that the process results in improved academic achievement for all students. Although the challenges to implementation are numerous, the focus on developing an integrated model of instruction, early intervention, and assessment to support student learning gives educators an opportunity to align and focus their efforts on ensuring appropriate learning experiences for all students. Over the course of the first year of implementation, Cheyenne Mountain has witnessed great success with its initiation of the RTI framework. The systematic process of the RTI framework provides an opportunity to align instruction, assessment, and interventions on the basis of individual student needs, to routinely evaluate its impact on student achievement, and to communicate more openly with parents.

REFERENCES

Colorado Student Assessment Program. (2006). *Colorado Student Assessment Program, Summary Report, 2005–06.* Colorado State Department of Education.

Deshler, D., Hock, M., & Catts, H. (2006). Enhancing outcomes for struggling adolescent readers. *IDA Perspectives.* Retrieved September 26, 2007, from http://www.ldonline.org/article/11768

Deshler, D. D., & Schumaker, J. B. (2006). *High school students with disabilities: Strategies for accessing the curriculum.* New York: Corwin Press.

Donovan, S., & Cross, C. T. (2002). *Minority students in special and gifted education.* Washington, DC: National Research Council, Committee on Minority Representation in Special Education.

DuFour, R., & Eaker, R. E. (1998). *Professional learning communities at work: Best practices for enhancing student achievement.* Bloomington, IN: National Education Service.

Fuchs, D., Mock, D., Morgan, P. L., & Young, C. L. (2003). Responsiveness-to-intervention: Definitions, evidence, and implications for the learning disabilities construct. *Learning Disabilities Research and Practice, 18*(3), 157–171.

Fuchs, L. S., & Fuchs, D. (2006). Implementing responsiveness-to-intervention to identify learning disabilities. *Perspectives, 32*(1), 39–43.

Greene, J. F. (1999). *Language! The comprehensive literacy curriculum.* (2nd ed.). Longmont, CO: Sopris West.

Johnson, E., Mellard, D. F., Fuchs, D., & McKnight, M. A. (2006). *Responsiveness to intervention (RTI): How to do it.* Lawrence, KS: National Research Center.

Kovaleski, J. (2003, December). *The three tier model of identifying learning disabilities: Critical program features and system issues.* Paper presented at the National Research Center on Learning Disabilities Responsiveness-to-Intervention Symposium, Kansas City, MO.

McMaster, K. L., Fuchs, D., Fuchs, L. & Compton, D. L. (2005). Responding to nonresponders: An experimental field trial of identification and intervention methods. *Exceptional Children, 71,* 445–463.

Mellard, D. F., & Johnson, E. S. (2008). *RTI: A practitioner's guide to implementing response-to-intervention.* Thousand Oaks, CA: Corwin Press.

Morris, J. D., Ehren, B. J., & Lenz, B. K. (1991). Building a model to predict which 4–8th graders will drop out of high school. *Journal of Experimental Education, 59,* 286–293.

Scantron. (2007). Performance series SM: Computer adaptive Internet assessment for schools. Retrieved September 26, 2007, from http://www.edperformance.com

Sugai G., Horner, R., & Gresham, F. (2002). Behaviorally effective school environments. In M. Shinn, H. Walker, & G. Stoner (Eds.), *Interventions for academic and behavior problems II: Preventive and remedial approach* (pp. 315–350). Bethesda, MD: Bethesda School of Psychologists.

Swanson, H. L. (2001). Research on interventions for adolescents with learning disabilities: A meta-analysis of outcomes related to higher-order processing. *Elementary School Journal, 101,* 331–348.

Vaughn, S. (2003, December). *How many tiers are needed for response to intervention to achieve acceptable prevention outcomes?* Paper presented at the National Research Center on Learning Disabilities Responsiveness-to-Intervention Symposium, Kansas City, MO. Retrieved March 15, 2006, from http://www.nrcld.org/symposium2003/vaughn/index.html

Originally published in *TEACHING Exceptional Children*, Vol. 40, No. 3, pp. 46–52.

11

English Language Learners and Response to Intervention: Referral Considerations

Claudia Rinaldi and Jennifer Samson

When a school is implementing a response to intervention model, what are the special considerations for the assessment of and referral for special education services for English language learners with academic difficulties? An RTI model and evidence-based instruction can inform the three areas of prereferral, referral, and assessment, as well as IEP development, for ELLs—but the assessment team must understand how to use information on oral language proficiency and academic language in the process. There are specific, appropriate action steps for educators during each phase of the process that will ensure that this group of students with unique learning needs are appropriately assessed and serviced.

As the number of English language learner (ELL) students in the U.S. grows, so does the need for guidelines on how best to address their educational needs. Although approximately 14% of the total school age population in the U.S. was identified as students with disabilities in the 2003 to 2004 school year (U.S. Department of Education, 2005), the proportion of ELLs with disabilities is unclear due to questions relating to data collected during the referral and assessment of this population. In fact, recent research suggests that schools are having a very difficult time distinguishing between the difficulty of acquiring a second language and a language-based learning disability (Klingner & Harry, 2006; Lesaux, 2006; McCardle, Mele-McCarthy, Cutting, Leos, & D'Emilio, 2005; Wagner, Francis, and Morris, 2005). Research also indicates that schools lack both a comprehensive approach to assessing ELLs and appropriate professional development for their personnel (Figueroa & Newsome, 2006; Klingner & Harry; Madaus, Rinaldi, Bigaj, & Chafouleas, in press; Sanchez & Brisk, 2004). Furthermore, schools across the country report inadequate services to address the unique learning needs of ELLs with disabilities (Zehler, Fleischman, Hopstock, Pendzick, & Stephenson, 2003).

New guidelines for school districts under the Individuals With Disabilities Education Improvement Act (IDEA) of 2004 recommend using evidence-based interventions—such as those utilized in a response to intervention (RTI) model—as diagnostic tools and as part of the identification and eligibility decision-making process for special education services and, in particular, for identifying learning disabilities (Mandlawitz, 2007). An RTI model integrates a multitier preventive instructional system (see Figure 1) and specifies the systematic use of a data-driven decision process to enhance outcomes for all children (Burns & VanDerHeyden, 2006). The President's Commission on Excellence in Special Education (2001) and the National Research Council's report on minority students (2002) also endorse RTI models for enhancing reading outcomes for ELLs.

WHEN DO YOU REFER AN ELL STUDENT FOR SPECIAL EDUCATION?

Many teachers delay referring ELL students for special education in order to provide the student ample opportunity to learn English (Limbos & Geva, 2002). However, if an ELL student does have a disability, early identification and intervention are essential. Waiting until fourth grade to identify reading difficulties makes remediation more challenging (Foorman, Francis, Shaywitz, Shaywitz, & Fletcher, 1997; Juel, 1988). Using scientifically based interventions in a RTI model with ELLs can improve the early literacy skills and overall reading outcomes for these students (Linan-Thompson, Cirino, & Vaughn, 2007). Kamps et al. (2007) reported that using a three-tiered RTI model (with Tier 2 addressing the needs of ELLs in small group instruction) resulted in higher gains than English as a second language (ESL) instruction alone.

The small group instruction of at-risk learners is a prereferral intervention that can significantly impact students' educational outcomes and reduce the number of students being referred for special education. It also assists in the diagnostic data collection process for referring those students who do not respond to intervention for special education assessment and services. Tier 2 also includes continued monthly progress monitoring to track learning rates and levels of performance attained during a defined timeline. It is vital that the ELL specialist, using informal measures, is also collecting data and tracking oral language skills and academic language (i.e., comprehension and vocabulary) development of ELL students. If the ELL student doesn't respond to instruction in Tier 2, the prereferral team can refer the student for possible special education eligibility and additional services and implement a Tier 3 intervention. Data collected during progress monitoring can inform decision

Figure 1. Response to Intervention Model for English Language Learners

Response to Intervention Model for English Language Learners

Referral to Special Ed.

TIER 3 One-on-One

Prereferral Intervention

TIER 2 Additional EIRP

Universal Screening

TIER 1 Evidenced-Based Instructional Reading Program (EIRP)

Increasing Needs-Based Intervention

Tier 3 – Tertiary Prevention
- 1:1 and PM
- MDT evaluation (IAP)
- Eligibility and IEP
  - Oral English proficiency and academic language proficiency
  - Monthly PM
  - Strategy interventions

Tier 2 – Small Group Tutoring
- 15–20 week sessions and weekly PM
- RTI base on 4 to 6 data points
- Add, change and/or refer

Tier 1 – Primary Prevention
- Universal screening (CBM probes) of all students
- Progress monitoring of ELLs: oral language proficiency and academic language proficiency
- Progress monitoring of high-risk students

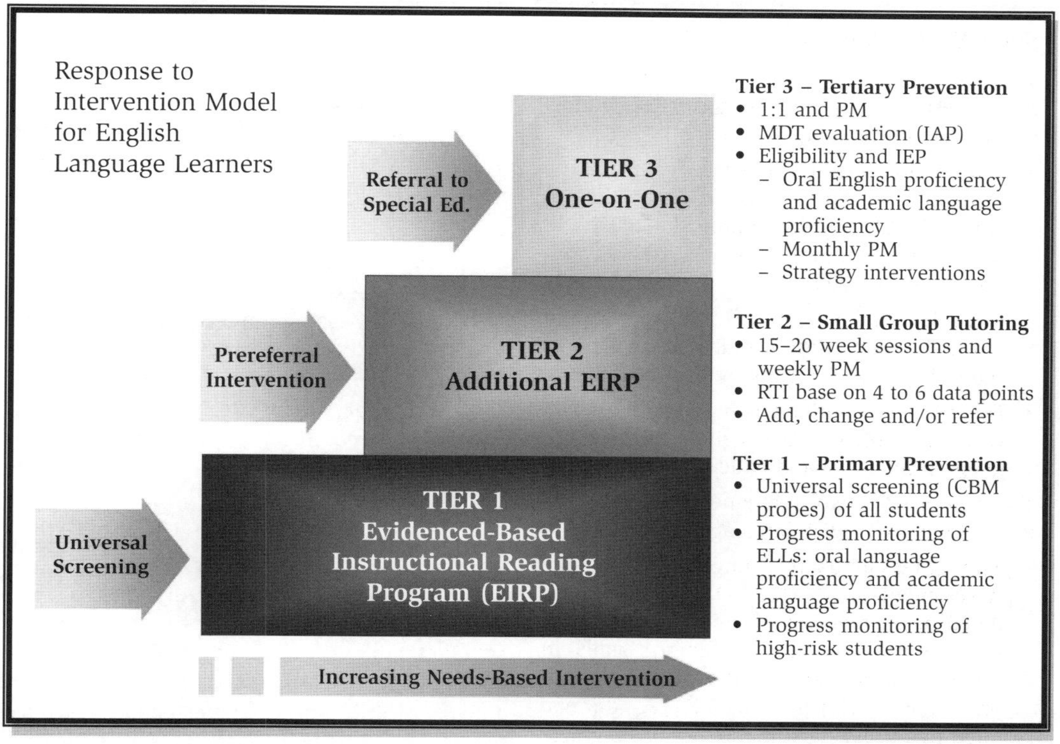

Note. CBM = curriculum-based measurement; ELL = English language learner; PM = progress monitoring; RTI = response to intervention; MDT = multidisciplinary team; IAP = individualized assessment plan; IEP = individualized education program.

making during the assessment and eligibility process (see sidebar, "Samuel: A Case Study).

The special education referral process begins when students do not respond appropriately to a Tier 2 instructional change. During the referral phase, general education teachers play an important role in ensuring that ELLs have had adequate evidence-based instruction as supported by the progress monitoring data, and in summarizing student progress for the multidisciplinary team (MDT). Special educators, ELL teachers, and parents can serve as consultants to general educators on whether academic difficulties reflect poor English proficiency, a transition to academic language development, or a possible learning disability in terms of performance rate and level of performance. Under the federal regulations of IDEA and the No Child Left Behind Act of 2001, students must be provided with high quality, evidence-based methods of instruction such as those used in a RTI model. Thus, in order to comply with federal regulations (see Mandlawitz, 2007), the MDT must evaluate the results of this instruction and the status of language

Samuel: A Case Study

Samuel's Elementary School

The Lake Shore School is currently implementing a response to intervention (RTI) model schoolwide for reading. The school:

1. Universally screens all students using the Dynamic Indicators of Basic Early Literacy Skills (DIBELS; Good & Kaminski, 2002) and the Developmental Reading Assessment (DRA; Beaver, 2003).

2. Identifies students at high, moderate, and low risk using DIBELS oral reading fluency (ORF) benchmarks (Good & Kaminski, 2002).

3. For students identified as high and moderate risk on DIBELS, collects their English language proficiency and educational history.

The school uses two assessments in establishing a student's English language proficiency:

1. The Massachusetts English Language Assessment-Oral (MELA-O), a state-mandated assessment of listening (comprehension) and speaking (production) skills in English for students with limited English proficiency (LEP) in Grades K–12, administered by observing students performing academic and social tasks in the classroom over a period of time.

2. The Massachusetts English Proficiency Assessment-Reading/Writing (MEPA-R/W), which assesses LEP students' proficiency in reading and writing at grade spans (Grades 3–4, 5–6, 7–8, and 9–12).

Lake Shore School provides support within the RTI model for reading instruction in 90-min blocks as follows:

1. Tier 1 students (scoring at grade level on DIBELS September benchmark and DRA grade-level equivalency) in Grades K–2 receive Fundations®: Wilson Language Basics (Wilson, 2005).

2. Tier 2 students (identified as moderate and high risk on DIBELS September benchmark assessment and below grade level of DRA) are separated into two groups:

   a. Students previously identified as receiving special education services.

   b. Students in beginning levels of English language proficiency according to the MELA-O and the MEPA.

Tier 2 students receive small group instruction using the Great Leaps Reading program (Mercer & Campbell, 1997).

3. Tier 3 students identified with a learning disabilities receive one-on-one support from the special education staff using Project Read® Multisensory Program (Greene & Enfield, 2006). Students who are as low-level ELLs receive Fundations®: Wilson Language Basics, Great Leaps Reading, and Project Read® interventions by regular education faculty and staff typically in small groups of 2–4 students at a time.

Samuel

Samuel is a student from South America who came to the United States 3 years ago; he has attended public school since age 5. He has three younger siblings. At home, his family speaks only Spanish; he speaks Spanish and English at school. He has many friends and is well liked by his teachers.

Samuel's classroom teacher describes him as

> a bright young boy who is very enthusiastic about learning. He works very hard in class in learning how to read and loves to see his progress when working with the Great Leaps Reading Program. We have seen progress, but in comparison to other students from Latino backgrounds and with similar immigration status, oral language proficiency, reading level, socioeconomic status and Spanish language use at home, his progress on the [curriculum-based assessment] has been slow to attain100% success with each lesson in Great Leaps. In monthly DIBELS check he has progressed slower than comparable peers.

continues

Samuel: A Case Study - *Continued*

Samuel's teachers are concerned that his progress is slower than anticipated and think he could benefit from additional support. Table A summarizes Samuel's curriculum-based assessment (CBA) progress scores and interventions within the school's RTI model; Figure A provides a summary of the CBA data.

The Special Education Assessment

Because Lake Shore School's prereferral team decided that Samuel's relatively slow growth in oral reading fluency might not be an English language proficiency issue, it requested an assessment by the school's special education team. The special education team decided on using native language and English assessments tools with low verbal requirements whenever possible. Table B details the tests and assessment tools used by the team.

Lake Shore School consequently found Samuel eligible for special education support based on CBA oral reading fluency progress within the RTI model and supporting results from the achievement and intellectual formal assessments. In April 2007, Samuel began to receive (in addition to Tier 1 and Tier 2 instruction) Tier 3 instruction using Project Read® Multisensory Program with ESL support.

Table A. Samuel's Curriculum-Based Assessment Profile Within the School's RTI Model

Time Period	Assessment	School Response	Observations/Interviews
September 2006	Schoolwide universal screening DRA - Level 16 DIBELS ORF - 01 MELA-O - Level 2 MEPA - R/W - Level 2	Identified as high risk Student selected for Tier 2 intervention Begins receiving Great Leaps Reading program (Mercer, & Campbell, 1997)	Observation evaluates academic engaged time in a typical reading lesson and center interaction. Results compared to a peer at the same ELL level and reading level as per ORF.
October 2006	Monthly progress monitoring DIBELS ORF - 08	Prereferral team evaluates progress monitoring results and classrooms observation and decides that the student is progressing very slowly. Team recommends additional ESL support during guided reading and literacy centers in addition to Great Leaps Reading (still within the Tier 2 level) If at a 6-week reevaluation progress is similar and additional ESL strategies and support are not impacting ORF, team will refer student for special education evaluation.	
November 2006	Monthly progress monitoring DIBELS ORF - 21		

continues

Samuel: A Case Study - *Continued*

Table A. *Continued*

Time Period	Assessment	School Response	Observations/Interviews
December 2006	Monthly progress monitoring DIBELS ORF - 29		Reevaluation of oral language proficiency and reading and writing English proficiency for gains since the beginning of the year.
			Interval recording, conducted twice, to evaluate language interactions in English and Spanish with teacher and peers looking for "positive," "negative," or "difficult to understand," and whether they were academic or social in nature.
			Parent interview in their primary language about how they thought the student was doing in school and the type of literacy supports he received at home and in which language.
January 2007	Monthly progress monitoring DIBELS ORF - 31		
February 2007	Monthly progress monitoring DIBELS ORF - 33 Schoolwide universal screening DRA - Level 18	Follow-up preferral team meeting recognizes that Samuel is gaining oral reading fluency but at the same rate. Team refers Samuel for a full referral to the special education team. Informal data, teacher, and parents interviews collected up to this time will be forwarded to the special education team.	

Note. DRA = Developmental Reading Assessment (Beaver, 2003); DIBELS ORF = Dynamic Indicators of Basic Early Literacy Skills Oral Reading Fluency (Good & Kaminski, 2002); MELA-O = Massachusetts English Language Assessment-Oral; MEPA-R/W = Massachusetts English Proficiency Assessment-Reading/Writing; ELL = English language learner; ESL = English as a second language.

continues

Samuel: A Case Study - *Continued*

Table B. Special Education Assessment Tools

Intellectual ability	Wechsler Intelligence Scale for Children (WISC; Wechsler, 2003)
	Woodcock Language Proficiency Battery (Woodcock, 1991)
	Bateria III Pruebas de Habilidades Cognitivas (Spanish; Woodcock, Muñoz-Sandoval, McGrew, & Mather, 2004a)
Achievement and academic language	Wechsler Individual Achievement Test (WIAT; English; Wechsler, 2001)
	Bateria III Pruebas de Aprovechamiento (Spanish; Woodcock, Muñoz-Sandoval, McGrew, & Mather, 2004b)
Phonological awareness	Comprehensive Test of Phonological Awareness (CTOPP; English and Spanish version; Wagner, Torgesen, & Rashotte, 1999)
Language proficiency/ interpersonal language	Woodcock Language Proficiency Battery-R (Spanish and English; Woodcock, 1991)
Family, educational, and medical interview	Family interview, educational history, family composition, migration and acculturation, goals for child, cultural difference, etc.
Classroom informal assessment	Measure of discrete gaps in the curriculum taught.

Figure A. Samuel's Curriculum-Based Assessment Progress Monitoring

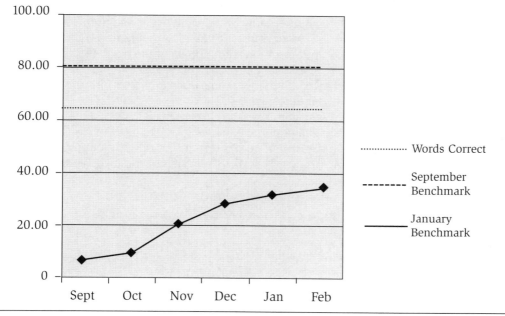

proficiency at each tier and decide whether the struggling ELL student received adequate instruction and intervention prior to referral for special education assessment.

Table 1 presents some questions to consider during this phase to help discern the differences and commonalities between and across oral language versus academic language versus learning disabilities. (Also see sidebar, "Samuel: A Case Study.") If the answers to these questions suggest that the ELL's needs were not addressed within the context of the general education program, school professionals must identify whether English language strategies with curriculum-based assessment (CBA) practices should be tried in an additional prereferral strategy or whether a full referral process should be conducted.

WHAT HAPPENS AFTER YOU REFER AN ELL STUDENT FOR A SPECIAL EDUCATION EVALUATION?

Once students are referred for a full special education evaluation, the several school professionals who comprise the MDT begin the development of the individualized assessment plan (IAP). The MDT has 60 days to complete the IAP and hold the eligibility and decision-making meeting (Mandlawitz, 2007; see also sidebar, "Samuel: A Case Study"). Throughout this process, the team needs to ensure that several federal requirements are met.

Tests and Other Evaluation Materials Should Not Be Racially or Culturally Biased

Test administrators should know whether the test was normed on a population that included students similar to the child being tested and whether the test items are appropriate and meaningful given the child's racial and cultural background and prior educational experiences. Test administrators also should select from a variety of assessment tools that can better inform the process for the individual ELL student.

For example, test administrators assessing an ELL student with a low level of English language proficiency need to decide whether an assessment tool that carries a significant verbal response mode is an appropriate choice, or whether one with lower verbal requirements would be better.

Tests and Other Evaluation Materials Should Be Administered in the Child's Native Language or Other Mode of Communication, When Possible

When assessing in the child's native language or in English, be aware that (a) many of the tests are not comparable, (b) the tasks may not be fully understood from the child's prior educational experiences, (c) the English language proficiency of each ELL is different and may provide a more or less predictive

Table 1. Preferral Considerations for English Language Learners

RTI Tier	Interpersonal English Language Acquisition Difficulties?	Academic Language Difficulties?	Learning Disability?
1	• What is the student's level of interpersonal English language proficiency? • What is the student's interpersonal native language proficiency? • Have bilingual education or ESL personnel made recommendations (Ortiz & Yates, 2001)? If so, are these recommendations being monitored using informal measures?		
2		• Is the student receiving instruction that addresses his language needs based on bilingual or ESL professional recommendations? • What is the rate of progress and level of English language proficiency since implementation of ESL instructional strategies (Ortiz & Yates 2001)? • What is the student's academic language proficiency? • What is the student's rate and level of reading and comprehension in the native language compared to English?	
3			• Has the student received evidence-based instruction and intervention to meet his academic needs? • Is there evidence of failure to respond to intervention (learning rate and level of performance)? • Is the data-driven progress monitoring addressing the student's needs effectively in the native language and in English?

Note. ESL = English as a second language.

level of learning, and (d) in many cases the assessment does not explicitly test what has been taught in the student's instructional history (Wagner et al., 2005). Caution should also be used when interpreting test results. Formal tests can provide valuable information about the individual's skills in the academic knowledge and language that can be used as a comparison tool to the normed population or to establish a discrepancy. For example, a test administrator using the results of a standardized tool that evaluates Spanish speakers outside of the United States should take into account the educational experiences of those children in contrast with the experiences of ELL students in the U.S.

Materials and Procedures Should Measure the Child's Potential Disability and Special Education Needs

It is important that the referral team select various data collection tools that assess different areas of development (academic, interpersonal, and language) in order to obtain a comprehensive picture of the student's ability level in oral language proficiency, basic reading skills (phonemic awareness, phonics, fluency, vocabulary and comprehension), and response to intervention (see sidebar, "Informal Tools for Assessing English Language Learners"). Depending on the program, any or all of these can be conducted in the child's primary language or in English and compared. A comprehensive and thorough data collection process that includes various tools and assessment (formal and informal) in appropriate language(s) assists the MDT in evaluating the "whole child" and deciding whether the weaknesses observed and tested are attributable to inadequate instruction, limited English proficiency, a learning disability, or a combination of these.

A Variety of Assessment Tools and Strategies Should Collect Functional and Developmental Information

No single procedure should be used as the only criterion to determine whether a child has a disability or to determine an appropriate educational program for the child (see sidebar, "Recommendations for Additional MDT Information Gathering"). Information from the parent(s) can provide functional, developmental, cultural, and linguistic information; the team should be aware of different cultural differences and experiences in prior schooling as well as family medical history, its immigration, and its acculturation. Parents can also provide information about how the child differs from other children in the home and assist in the evaluation of English proficiency when appropriate. MDT professionals should also gather information from the parents about their goals for their child's English-language education and their choice in maintaining their native language.

Informal Tools for Assessing English Language Learners

> ✔ *Curriculum-based assessment* is the process of determining students' instructional needs within a curriculum by directly assessing specific curriculum skills (Choate, Enright, Miller, Poteet, Rakes (1995).
>
> ✔ *Classroom tests* refers to the procedure of selecting content from the curriculum to be assessed (McLoughlin & Lewis, 2005).
>
> ✔ *Informal inventories* are screening devices on selected parts of the curriculum, typically reading decoding or comprehension (McLoughlin & Lewis, 2005).
>
> ✔ *Classroom targeted observations* refers to continuous recording, sequence analysis, and work sample analysis (McLoughlin & Lewis, 2005).
>
> ✔ *Error analysis* records additions, omissions, substitutions, repetitions and so forth (McLoughlin & Lewis, 2005).
>
> ✔ *Dynamic assessment* refers to a test, teach, and retest method to examine the learner's strategies (McLoughlin & Lewis, 2005).
>
> ✔ *Task analysis* refers to isolating a behavior into a skill sequence to establish the learner's skill status within the behavior (McLoughlin & Lewis, 2005).
>
> ✔ *Diagnostic probes* are procedures that evaluate whether, when some aspect of the classroom task is changed, it will have a positive effect on student performance (McLoughlin & Lewis, 2005).
>
> ✔ *Diagnostic teaching* refers to a procedure of investigating the relative effectiveness of two or more instructional techniques (McLoughlin & Lewis, 2005).

The Child Should Be Assessed in All Areas of Suspect Disability

Health, vision, hearing, social, emotional, and motor should be assessed in the dominant language. General intelligence, academic performance, communicative status, and language acquisition should be assessed using more than one tool in the student's native language and in English, if appropriate.

DEVELOPING AN INDIVIDUALIZED EDUCATION PROGRAM FOR AN ELL STUDENT WITH A DISABILITY

The individualized education program (IEP) development phase begins once the assessment, eligibility, and decision-making process is complete. The IEP of an ELL needs to address (a) disability eligibility, (b) present level and rate of performance in the academic curriculum, (c) specialized instruction

Recommendations for Additional Information Gathering

✔ Interviews of family for medical and educational background

✔ Work samples (oral language and narrative)

✔ Review of educational, cultural, and family records

✔ Observations at home and school

✔ Consultation with other individuals familiar with child in school and community

✔ Linguistic demands in native and English languages in the home community

including goals that focus on increasing the child's rate of learning and English language acquisition, and (d) accommodation and adaptations used in the classroom and in statewide testing.

Develop a Comprehensive Summary of the Student's Skills

This includes functional, linguistic, and academic skills, progress in the classroom, and current ability in and out of the classroom. The results should clearly identify which assessment tools were given and in which language and whether they are a reliable representation of the student's ability or if language could have potentially interfered in the results and scoring. To accomplish this, the assessment process should include the child's educational history, years in the U.S., and type of instructional program. (For example, noting transitional/early exit program vs. sheltered english instruction vs. two-way bilingual education programs.)

Provide Report Results Prior to the IEP Team Meeting

A short summary of various report results permits the IEP team members to read them carefully and prepare for the development meeting. The team should focus on the particular needs of the child and not simply on programs currently available in the school. Language of instruction should be carefully considered, as the goal is to provide access to the general curriculum.

Identify Scientifically Based Instructional Practices and Progress Monitoring

Within the RTI model, ELL students with identified disabilities and an IEP continue receiving instruction in the regular curriculum, plus a Tier 2 program and special education services through Tier 3. School professionals

Recommended Professional Development Topics

> ✔   Appropriate formal and informal evaluation practices
>
> ✔   Understanding and evaluating second language acquisition
>
> ✔   Matching instructional strategies at each stage of language development
>
> ✔   Typical and atypical language and literacy characteristics of ELLs
>
> ✔   Accommodations and adaptations during testing situations for ELLs
>
> ✔   Accommodations and adaptations for the classroom
>
> ✔   Collaboration with colleagues
>
> ✔   Eligibility determination
>
> ✔   Progress monitoring

delivering the instructions should be assisted in order to ensure proper intervention and progress monitoring as needed, through coaching or professional development.

Provide Professional Development to All Teachers Involved

All teachers implementing the RTI service model with ELL students need experience and training on a variety of topics (see sidebar, "Recommended Professional Development Topics")—and in two languages, in a two-way or other type of bilingual program. For sheltered English programs, the team should discuss the impact of not supporting the child's native language and its possible impact on rate of growth in oral language proficiency and academic language development.

Enhance Logistics

Use a tracking mechanism to ensure that all documentation is in the child's records in an organized and comprehensive manner and available for all school-based professionals working with the ELL.

Develop a Collaborative Team

Those who best know the child should be considered of equal value as any other member of the team and can inform others about the student's progress in the attainment of goals and objectives of academic skills in various settings and in various languages. Developing a collaborative team effort increases the attendance of all stakeholders (particularly parents) at meetings and encourages them to be active participants in the decision-making process of the special education referral team.

Develop a Plan for Implementing Accommodations and Modifications

The plan for accommodations and modifications, both in the classroom and for statewide testing, needs to be one that can feasibly be addressed and supported by the general education teacher and special education staff.

FINAL THOUGHTS

The most salient difficulty in assessing ELL students who exhibit academic difficulties is identifying whether the problem is one of English proficiency or of a learning disability. In many cases the symptoms are shared and difficult to disentangle, but obtaining a comprehensive picture of the child is vital for disability eligibility (Rhodes, Ochoa, & Ortiz, 2005; Salend & Salinas, 2003). The RTI model provides an additional source of information during the special education referral process, using data-driven CBA in conjunction with scientifically based instruction. All school professionals addressing the needs of children who are having academic difficulties will be involved in more meaningful ways during progress monitoring and evaluation of eligibility for special education.

This article discusses the prereferral and referral assessment and IEP development for ELLs within an RTI model, providing a framework for integrating the results from the bilingual ESL specialist, the classroom teachers, and the MDT. We suggest questions and approaches to help guide the team in addressing ESL instructional recommendations for a student's English language proficiency and academic difficulties in the general education classroom and in integrating formal assessments with information on progress monitoring and ESL services when making IEP recommendations. Integrating formal and informal assessment information throughout the tiers results in more effective development of IEP goals, collaboration efforts among the MDT, and support for the connections that establish the rate and level of learning with attainable and measurable goals for students eligible for special education services, Limitations and difficulties in identifying ELLs as limited language proficient or having a learning disability may continue, but following these recommendations allows professionals to be better informed and make decisions that address continuous progress monitoring and scientifically based instructional programming.

REFERENCES

Beaver, J. (2003). *Developmental reading assessment*. Parsippany, NJ: Celebration Press.

Burns, M. K., & VanderHeyden, A. M. (2006). Using response to intervention to assess learning disabilities. *Assessment for Effective Intervention, 32*(1), 3–5.

Choate, J. S., Enright, B. E., Miller, L. J., Poteet, J. A., & Rakes, T. A. (1995). *Curriculum-based assessment and programming*. Needham Heights, MA: Allyn & Bacon.

Figueroa, R. A., & Newsome, P. (2006). The diagnosis of LD in English learners: Is it nondiscriminatory? *Journal of Learning Disabilities, 39*, 206–214.

Foorman, B., Francis, D., Shaywitz, S. E., Shaywitz, B., & Fletcher, J. M. (1997). The case for early reading intervention. In B. Blachman (Ed.), *Foundations of reading acquisition and dyslexia: Implications for early intervention* (pp. 243–264). Mahwah, NJ: Lawrence Erlbaum.

Good, R. H., & Kaminski, R. A. (2002). *Dynamic indicators of basic early literacy skills* (6th ed.) Eugene, OR: Institute for the Development of Educational Achievement.

Greene, V., & Enfield, M. (2006). *Project Read®*. Bloomington, MN: Language Circle Enterprises.

Juel, C. (1988). Learning to read and write: A longitudinal study of 54 children from first through fourth grades. *Journal of Educational Psychology, 80*, 437–447.

Kamps, D., Abbott, M., Greenwood, C., Arreaga-Mayer, C., Wills, H., Lonstaff, J., et al. (2007). Use of evidenced-based, small group reading instruction for English language learners in elementary grades: Secondary-tier intervention. *Learning Disabilities Quarterly, 30*, 163–168.

Klingner, J. K., & Harry, B. (2006). The special education referral and decision-making process for English language learners: Child study team meetings and staffings. *Teachers College Record, 108*, 2247–2281.

Lesaux, N. K. (2006). Building consensus: Future directions for research on English language learners at risk for learning difficulties. *Teachers College Record, 108*, 2406–2438.

Limbos, M., & Geva, E. (2002). Accuracy of teacher assessments of second-language students at risk for reading disability. *Journal of Learning Disabilities, 34*, 137–151.

Linan-Thompson, S., Cirino, P. T., & Vaughn, S. (2007). Determining English language learners' response to intervention: Questions and some answers. *Learning Disability Quarterly, 30*, 185–195.

Madaus, J., Rinaldi, C., Bigaj, S., & Chafouleas, S. (in press). Use of assessment instruments and techniques in local school districts. *Assessment for Effective Intervention.*

Mandlawitz, M. (2007). *What every teacher should know about IDEA laws and regulations.* Boston: Pearson.

McCardle, P., Mele-McCarthy, J., Cutting, L., Leos, K., & D'Emilio, T. (2005). Learning disabilities in English language learners: Identifying the issues. *Learning Disabilities Research and Practice, 20*, 1–5.

McLoughlin, J.A. & Lewis, R. B. (2005). *Assessing students with special needs.* (6th ed.) Upper Saddle River, NJ: Prentice Hall.

Mercer, C. D., & Campbell, K. U. (1997). *Great leaps reading program.* Gainesville, FL: Diarmuid.

National Research Council (2002). *Minority students in special and gifted education.* Washington, DC: National Academy Press.

Ortiz, A. A., & Yates, J. R. (2001). A framework for serving English language learners with disabilities. *The Journal of Special Education, 14*, 72–80.

President's Commission on Excellence in Special Education. (2001). *A new era: Revitalizing special education for children and their families.* Washington, DC: U.S. Department of Education.

Rhodes, R., Ochoa, S., & Ortiz, S. (2005). *Assessing culturally and linguistically diverse students.* New York: Guilford Publications.

Salend, S. J., & Salinas, A (2003). Language differences or learning difficulties: The work of the multidisciplinary team. *TEACHING Exceptional Children, 35*(4), 36–43.

Sanchez, M., & Brisk, M. (2004). Teacher's assessment practices and understandings in a bilingual program. *NABE Journal of Research and Practice, 2*(1), 193–208.

U.S. Department of Education. (2005). *Digest of education statistics, 2004* (NCES 2006-05). Retrieved August 5, 2006, from http://nces.ed.gov/fastfacts/display.asp?id = 64

Wagner, R., Torgesen, J., & Rashotte, C. (1999). *Comprehensive test of phonological processing.* Austin, TX: Pro-Ed.

Wagner, R. K., Francis, D. J., & Morris, R. D. (2005). Identifying English language learners with learning disabilities: Key challenges and possible approaches. *Learning Disabilities Research and Practice, 20*(1), 17–23.

Wechsler, D. (2003). *Wechsler intelligence scale for children* (4th ed.). San Antonio, TX: Psychological Corporation.

Wechsler, D. (2001). *Wechsler individual achievement test.* San Antonio: TX: Psychological Corporation.

Wilson Language Training. (2005). *Fundations®*. Oxford, MA: Wilson Language Training Corporation.

Woodcock, R. W. (1991). *Woodcock language proficiency battery-revised.* Chicago: Riverside.

Woodcock, R. W., Munoz-Sandoval, A. F., McGrew, K. S., & Mather, N. (2004a). *Bateria III Woodcock-Munoz pruebas de aprovechamiento - Revisados.* Itasca, IL: Riverside.

Woodcock, R. W., Munoz-Sandoval, A. F., McGrew, K. S., & Mather, N. (2004b). *Bateria III Woodcock-Munoz pruebas de habilidades cognitivas - Revisados.* Itasca, IL: Riverside.

Zehler, A. M., Fleischman, H. L., Hopstock, P. J., Pendzick, M. L., & Stephenson, T. G. (2003). *Descriptive study of services to LEP students and LEP students with disabilities.* (No. 4). Arlington, VA: U.S. Department of Education, Office of English Language Acquisition.

Originally published in *TEACHING Exceptional Children*, Vol. 40, No. 5, pp. 6–14.

12

RTI After IDEA:
A Survey of State Laws

Perry A. Zirkel and Nico Krohn

Touted as a more effective approach to determining eligibility for specific learning disability (SLD) than establishing a severe discrepancy between ability and achievement, response to intervention (RTI) represents various models that share these common characteristics: (a) multiple tiers of scientific, research-based interventions; (b) continuous progress monitoring; and (c) systematic decision points to screen students for an evaluation for special education (e.g., Batsche et al., 2001). The professional literature is replete with rhetoric and, to a lesser extent, research concerning implementing RTI.

IDEA LEGISLATION

Faced with a rising chorus from various influential individuals in the professional community to replace the severe discrepancy formula with RTI as the primary approach for determining eligibility, Congress compromised in the 2004 amendments to the Individuals With Disabilities Education Improvement Act (IDEA). Specifically, IDEA now disallows states from continuing to require the severe discrepancy approach and expressly permits school districts to use "a process which determines if a child responds to scientific, research-based intervention" (IDEA, §1414(b)(6)(A))—which amounts to RTI.

IDEA REGULATIONS

The 2006 IDEA regulations (§300.307(a)) require each state to choose its SLD eligibility "criteria" from among the following options:

(1) Severe discrepancy—may prohibit or permit

(2) RTI—must permit

(3) "Other alternative research-based procedures"—may permit

In a subsequent cross-reference to these three choices, the regulations repeat the RTI designation as "a process based on the child's response to scientific, research-based intervention" but conflate the other two options under the broad rubric of "a pattern of strengths and weaknesses in performance, achievement, or both, relative to age, State-approved grade-level standards, or intellectual development, that is determined by the group to be relevant to the identification of [SLD]" (IDEA regulations, 2006, §300.309(a)(2)).

The regulations do not define RTI beyond the aforementioned descriptive designation, but they require that if RTI is chosen, the eligibility evaluation report must include statements of the following:

(i) The instructional strategies used and the student-centered data collected; and

(ii) The documentation that the child's parents were notified about—

(A) The State's policies regarding the amount and nature of student performance data that would be collected and the general education services that would be provided;

(B) Strategies for increasing the child's rate of learning; and

(C) The parents' right to request an evaluation. (§300.311(a)(7))

Additionally, even if RTI is not chosen, the regulations require the eligibility team to "consider" in their evaluation continuous progress monitoring (a practice associated with RTI), described as "Data-based documentation of repeated assessments of achievement at reasonable intervals, reflecting formal assessment of student progress during instruction, . . . provided to the child's parents" (IDEA regulations, 2006, §300.309(b)(2)).

IDEA POLICY INTERPRETATIONS

In the commentary accompanying the IDEA regulations (2006), the U.S. Department of Education's Office of Special Education Programs (OSEP) appeared to reflect a pro-RTI attitude, as exemplified by this excerpt:

> Consensus reports and empirical syntheses indicate a need for major changes in the approach to identifying children with SLD. Models that incorporate RTI represent a shift in special education toward goals of better achievement and improved behavioral outcomes for children with SLD because the children who are identified under such models are most likely to require special education and related services. (p. 46,647)

At the same time, in light of the legislative framework, OSEP allowed for other options. The commentary (2006) provided this example of the third option of other alternative research-based procedures:

> A state could choose to identify children based on absolute low achievement and consideration of exclusionary factors as one criterion for eligibility. Other alternatives might combine features of different models for identification. (p. 46,648)

However, the commentary is not particularly enlightening as to the meaning of "pattern of strengths and weaknesses," merely stating that it commonly refers to "the examination of profiles across different tests used historically in the identification of children with SLD" (p. 46,654).

With regard to the requirement for notifying the parents about their right to an evaluation, the commentary (2006) explains:

> Models based on RTI typically evaluate the child's response to instruction prior to the onset of the 60-day period, and generally do not require as long a time to complete an evaluation because of the amount of data already collected on the child's achievement, including observation data (p. 46,658).

Finally, OSEP's policy guidance subsequent to the IDEA regulations provides the following interpretations:

(1) A state may use any combination of these three options (Letter to Zirkel, 2007).

(2) Eligibility criteria "should" be consistent across a state (Questions and answers, 2007).

(3) If a district chooses to gradually "scale up" the implementation of RTI, including   training staff, the district cannot use it for identification of children with SLD until fully implemented in the entire system (Questions and answers, 2007).

(4) RTI, severe discrepancy, and other alternative procedures are just one component of an overall comprehensive evaluation to determine SLD eligibility (Letter to Prifitera, 2007).

STATE LAWS

The IDEA regulations went into effect on October 12, 2006. What is the status of the resulting state laws 1 year later? Table 1 provides a snapshot summary based on the 47 usable responses from all 50 states that responded to our e-mail survey of state directors of special education, asking whether their state law was at the "proposed" stage (defined broadly to include official drafts) or finalized, and which choice the proposed or finalized state law has taken with regard to the three options under the IDEA regulations. (The table does not include entries for 3 of the 50 responding states; Alaska, New Hampshire, and New Jersey responded that they have not reached the stage of an identifiably proposed choice.)

Table 1 shows that 1 year after the effective date of the IDEA regulations, approximately half the states have not yet finalized their laws with regard to the status of RTI in the SLD eligibility process, and that the vast majority of the states have tended toward a permissive approach, effectively delegating the choice among RTI, severe discrepancy, and (in small subset of the states) a third research-based option. On the other hand, only a few states have opted to require RTI and prohibit severe discrepancy. Between these two groups of states falls a second small minority, a transitional group, moving toward effectively requiring RTI but neither as immediately nor to the same extent as the mandatory group. There is considerable variation within these categories, partially attributable to the ambiguity of "pattern of strengths and weaknesses" in the IDEA regulations and to the obvious difficulties of implementing such a comprehensive new approach.

Moreover, the boundaries of these categories and the entries within them are rather fluid. First, the proposed status of almost half of the states leaves open the foreseeable possibility of revision prior to finalization. Second, supplementary survey responses and other informal reports indicate that many states and districts in the predominant, permissive group of states are encouraging and experimenting with RTI, even if not formally requiring it. Finally, a few of the states are on the rather permeable borders of the three categories. For example, West Virginia is included in the mandatory group but it is transitional to the extent it will not prohibit severe discrepancy until June 30, 2009. Similarly, New Mexico and New York are in the permissive group but they too are transitional to a limited extent; New Mexico will require RTI as of July 1, 2009, in Grades K–2, and New York will prohibit severe discrepancy after July 10, 2012, for Grades K–4 in the reading areas.

Regardless of current category, the implementation of RTI, as the professional literature is now making clearer, is a major challenge, requiring a comprehensive commitment by general education and careful coordination with special education (Fuchs & Deshler, 2007; Gersten & Dimino, 2006; Zirkel, 2007). As Burns (2007) observed, "we have to recognize it as a *paradigmatic change* rather than a supposed innovation" (p. 39). Moreover, for the majority of states, which have opted for the permissive approach, school districts

Table 1. State Laws Regarding SLD Eligibility Determination: October 2007 (N = 47)

State's Choice Regarding RTI and Other Options	Proposed Stage (n = 23)	Finalized (n = 24)
Mandatory (6 states; 13%); require RTI and		
Prohibit SD	FL, IN	CO, WV[a]
Other variation		DE[b], GA[c]
Transitional (4 states; 9%)		
Permit RTI and third alternative but prohibit SD		IA
Permit RTI and—only until 2010—SD		IL, ME[d]
Permit all three options but intend to require RTI	LA	
Permissive (37 states; 79%); permit RTI and		
SD only	AZ, MN, MT, NE, NC, PA, RI, TX, WI	ID, MD, MO, ND, NM[e], NV, OK, OR[f], SD, VT, WA, WY
SD and third alternative	AR, CA, CT, HI, KY, MA, MI, OH[g], SC, VA	AL, KS, NY[h], TN
SD or combination of RTI-SD	MS	UT

Note. SLD = specific learning disability; RTI = response to intervention; SD = severe discrepancy.
[a] Permits SD until June 30, 2009.
[b] Provides alternative of "pattern of strengths and weaknesses."
[c] Provides for other information including SD-type data under "pattern of strengths and weaknesses."
[d] Requires RTI under label of "prereferral" by 2010.
[e] Requires RTI in Grades K–2 as of July 1, 2009.
[f] Subsumes SD under "patterns of strengths and weaknesses."
[g] Requires the state education agency to approve third option.
[h] Provides for third alternative in the form of "pattern of strengths and weaknesses" and prohibits SD for Grades K–4 in reading effective July 1, 2012.

will have various practical problems not only in terms of cross pressures from neighboring districts but also from parents of students coming from other districts and from private schools. Finally, from a legal perspective, simply providing lip service to RTI, rather than establishing defensible policies, practices, and documentation, is likely to reverse the pro-district trend of case law concerning SLD eligibility (Zirkel, 2006). Given the fluidity of state laws, the specific scope of this survey, and the need for a comprehensive eligibility evaluation in conformity with both federal and state requirements, careful examination of the particular provisions of individual state law is an essential step toward such defensibility.

REFERENCES

Batsche, G., et al. (2005). *Response to Intervention: Policy considerations and implementation.* Alexandria, VA: National Association of State Directors of Special Education.

Burns, M. K. (2007). RTI *will* fail, unless..., *Communiqué, 35*(5), 3–39.

Commentary accompanying IDEA regulations, 71 Fed. Reg. 46,540–46,753 (Aug. 14, 2006).

Fuchs, D., & Deshler, D. D. (2007). What we need to know about responsiveness to intervention (and shouldn't be afraid to ask). *Learning Disabilities Research & Practice, 22,* 129–136.

Gersten, R., & Dimino, J. A. (2006), RTI (Response to Intervention): Rethinking special education for students with reading difficulties (yet again). *Reading Research Quarterly, 41,* 99–107.

Individuals With Disabilities Education Improvement Act of 2004, 20 U.S.C. §§ 1401 *et seq.* (2005).

Letter to Prifitera, 48 IDELR ¶ 163 (OSEP 2007).

OSEP Letter to Zirkel, 48 IDELR ¶ 192 (OSEP 2007).

Questions and answers on response to intervention (RTI) and early intervening services (EIS), 47 IDELR ¶ 196 (OSEP 2007).

Regulations for the Individuals With Disabilities Education Act, 34 C.F.R. §§ 300.1 *et seq.* (2006).

Zirkel, P. (2006). *The legal meaning of specific learning disability for special education eligibility.* Arlington, VA: Council for Exceptional Children.

Zirkel, P. (2007). The pluses and perils of RTI, *School Administrator, 64*(4), 53–54.

Originally published in *TEACHING Exceptional Children,* Vol. 40, No. 3, pp. 71–73.